I0815292

The Way of the Cross

With the Saints

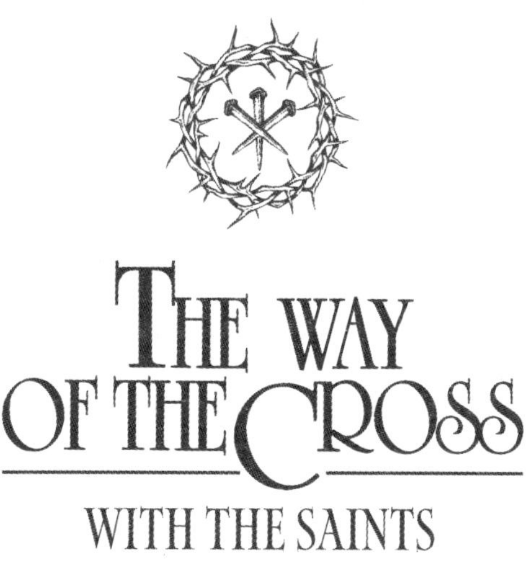

THE WAY OF THE CROSS WITH THE SAINTS

COMPILED BY TAN BOOKS

TAN BOOKS
GASTONIA, NORTH CAROLINA

This edition is a compilation of various sources published by TAN Books. These works under TAN Books' copyright include *Way of the Cross According to St. Francis of Assisi*, *Way of the Cross According to St. Alphonsus Liguori*, and *Stations of the Cross According to St. John Henry Cardinal Newman*.

All hymns in the Appendix are in the public domain via hymnary.org and openhymnal.org. The English translations of "Adore Te Devote" and "Pange Lingua" are by Edward Caswell.

Cover design by Jordan Avery

ISBN: 978-1-5051-3617-3
Kindle ISBN: 978-1-5051-3717-0
ePUB ISBN: 978-1-5051-3716-3

Published in the United States by
TAN Books
PO Box 269
Gastonia, NC 28053
www.TANBooks.com

Printed in India

CONTENTS

EDITOR'S NOTE

AS THIS WORLD GETS LOUDER, busier, and more focused on material things, it's simple for us to follow that fallen path toward despair. It's all too easy to forget our true journey and destination. But Our Lord calls us to listen, even amid the noise. He calls us to be still, even amid the storms. He calls us to carry our cross and follow Him.

The Way of the Cross or *Stations of the Cross* offers a unique opportunity for us to do just that. A solemn devotion that, as legend has it, was begun by Our Blessed Lady herself, *The Way of the Cross* has become a form of prayer and meditation beloved by many. The great saints all agree that meditation on the Passion and death of Our Lord is one of the most fruitful devotions one can pray.

In this special edition, we've compiled *The Way of the Cross* according to the methods of three spiritual masters: St. Francis of Assisi, St. Alphonsus Liguori, and St. John Henry Cardinal Newman, along with the mystical visions of Bl. Anne Catherine Emmerich and Ven. Mary of Jesus of Ágreda. Though similar in form and structure, these three distinct methods offer us special forms to meditate on the Passion of Our Lord. With these saints as our guide, we can begin our journey to breaking free from worldly things and self-centeredness. We can begin our journey to humility and meekness as we follow in the footsteps of Our Lord. We can begin to ease our restless hearts as we find our true rest in Him.

February 1
Feast of Saint Ansgar

THE WAY OF THE CROSS WITH THE SAINTS

Preparatory Prayer

Together: O most merciful Jesus, with a contrite heart and penitent spirit, I bow down in profound humility before Thy divine majesty. I adore Thee as my supreme Lord and Master; I believe in Thee, I hope in Thee, I love Thee above all things. I am heartily sorry for having offended Thee, my Supreme and Only Good. I resolve to amend my life, and although I am unworthy to obtain mercy, yet the sight of Thy holy cross, on which Thou didst die, inspires me with hope and consolation. I will, therefore, meditate on Thy sufferings and visit the stations of Thy Passion in company with Thy sorrowful Mother and my guardian angel, with the intention of promoting Thy honor and saving my soul.

I desire to gain all the indulgences granted for this holy exercise, for myself and for the Poor Souls in Purgatory. O merciful Redeemer, who hast said, "And I, if I be lifted from earth, will draw all things to Myself," draw my heart and my love to Thee, that I may perform this devotion as perfectly as possible, and that I may live and die in union with Thee. *Amen.*

Prayer to the Shoulder Wound of Jesus
(St. Bernard of Clairvaux)

St. Bernard asked Our Lord which was His greatest unrecorded suffering. Our Lord answered: "I had on My Shoulder, while I bore My Cross on the Way of Sorrows, a grievous Wound, which was more painful than the others and which is not recorded by men. Honor this Wound with thy devotion and I will grant thee whatsoever thou dost ask through Its virtue and merit. And in regard to all those who shall venerate this Wound, I will remit to them all their venial sins and will no longer remember their mortal sins."

The Prayer to the Shoulder Wound of Jesus

O Loving Jesus, meek Lamb of God, I, a miserable sinner, salute and worship the most Sacred Wound of Thy Shoulder, on which Thou didst bear Thy heavy Cross, which so tore Thy Flesh and laid bare Thy Bones as to inflict on Thee an anguish greater than any other Wound of Thy Most Blessed Body. I adore Thee, O Jesus most sorrowful; I praise and glorify Thee and give Thee thanks for this most sacred and painful Wound, beseeching Thee by that exceeding pain and by the crushing burden of Thy heavy Cross to be merciful to me, a sinner, to forgive me all my mortal and venial sins, and to lead me on towards Heaven along the Way of Thy Cross. Amen.

Pope Eugenius III, at the earnest request of St. Bernard, has granted three thousand years' Indulgence to all who, with a contrite heart, recite the Lord's Prayer and Hail Mary three times, in honor of the Wound on the Shoulder of Our Blessed Redeemer.

THE WAY OF THE CROSS

According to the Method of

ST. FRANCIS OF ASSISI

First Station

JESUS IS CONDEMNED TO DEATH

Stabat Mater dolorosa,
Juxta crucem lacrymosa,
Dum pendebat Filius.

FIRST STATION

JESUS IS CONDEMNED TO DEATH

V. We adore Thee, O Christ, and we praise Thee, (*Genuflect*)
R. Because by Thy holy cross Thou hast redeemed the world.

Priest: Jesus, most innocent, who neither did nor could commit a sin, was condemned to death, and moreover, to the most ignominious death of the cross. To remain a friend of Caesar, Pilate delivered Him into the hands of His enemies. A fearful crime—to condemn Innocence to death, and to offend God in order not to displease men.

People: O innocent Jesus, having sinned, I am guilty of eternal death, but Thou willingly does accept the unjust sentence of death, that I might live. For whom, then, shall I henceforth live, if not for Thee, my Lord? Should I desire to please men, I could not be Thy servant. Let me, therefore, rather displease men and all the world, than not please Thee, O Jesus.

Our Father. Hail Mary. Glory Be.

V. Lord Jesus, crucified,
R. Have mercy on us!

All: At the cross her station keeping,
Stood the mournful Mother weeping,
Close to Jesus to the last.

Second Station

JESUS IS MADE TO CARRY HIS CROSS

Cujus animam gementem,
Contristatam et dolentem,
Pertransivit gladius.

SECOND STATION

JESUS IS MADE TO CARRY HIS CROSS

V. We adore Thee, O Christ, and we praise Thee, (*Genuflect*)
R. Because by Thy holy cross Thou hast redeemed the world.

Priest: When our divine Savior beheld the cross, He most willingly stretched out His bleeding arms, lovingly embraced it, and tenderly kissed it, and placing it on His bruised shoulders, He, although almost exhausted, joyfully carried it.

People: O my Jesus, I cannot be Thy friend and follower, if I refuse to carry the cross. O dearly beloved cross! I embrace thee, I kiss thee, I joyfully accept thee from the hands of my God. Far be it from me to glory in anything, save in the cross of my Lord and Redeemer. By it the world shall be crucified to me, and I to the world, that I may be Thine forever.

Our Father. Hail Mary. Glory Be.

V. Lord Jesus, crucified,
R. Have mercy on us!

All: Through her heart, His sorrow sharing,
All His bitter anguish bearing,
Now at length the sword has passed.

Third Station

JESUS FALLS THE FIRST TIME

O quam tristis et afflicta
Fuit ilia benedicta
Mater Unigeniti!

THIRD STATION

JESUS FALLS THE FIRST TIME

V. We adore Thee, O Christ, and we praise Thee,
(*Genuflect*)
R. Because by Thy holy cross Thou hast redeemed the world.

Priest: Our dear Savior, carrying the cross, was so weakened by its heavy weight as to fall exhausted to the ground. Our sins and misdeeds were the heavy burden which oppressed Him: the cross was to Him light and sweet, but our sins were galling and insupportable.

People: O my Jesus, Thou did bear my burden and the heavy weight of my sins Should I, then, not bear in union with Thee, my easy burden of suffering and accept the sweet yoke of Thy commandments? Thy yoke is sweet and Thy burden is light: I therefore willingly accept it. I will take up my cross and follow Thee.

Our Father. Hail Mary. Glory Be.

V. Lord Jesus, crucified,
R. Have mercy on us!

All: O, how sad and sore distressed
Was that Mother highly blessed
Of the sole-begotten One!

Fourth Station

JESUS MEETS HIS SORROWFUL MOTHER

Quae moerebat, et dolebat,
Pia Mater dum videbat
Nati poenas inclyti.

FOURTH STATION

JESUS MEETS HIS SORROWFUL MOTHER

V. We adore Thee, O Christ, and we praise Thee, (*Genuflect*)
R. Because by Thy holy cross Thou hast redeemed the world.

Priest: How painful and how sad it must have been for Mary, the sorrowful Mother, to behold her beloved Son, laden with the burden of the cross! What unspeakable pangs her most tender heart experienced! How earnestly did she desire to die in place of Jesus, or at least with Him! Implore this sorrowful Mother that she assist you in the hour of your death.

People: O Jesus, O Mary, I am the cause of the great and manifold pains which pierce your loving hearts! O, that also my heart would feel and experience at least some of your sufferings! O, Mother of Sorrows, let me participate in the sufferings which thou and Thy Son endured for me, and let me experience thy sorrow, that afflicted with thee, I may enjoy thy assistance in the hour of my death.

Our Father. Hail Mary. Glory Be.

V. Lord Jesus, crucified,
R. Have mercy on us!

All: Christ above in torment hangs,
She beneath beholds the pangs
Of her dying, glorious Son.

Fifth Station

SIMON OF CYRENE HELPS JESUS TO CARRY HIS CROSS

Quis est homo qui non fleret
Matrem Christi si videret
In tanto supplicio?

FIFTH STATION

SIMON OF CYRENE HELPS JESUS TO CARRY HIS CROSS

V. We adore Thee, O Christ, and we praise Thee,
(Genuflect)
R. Because by Thy holy cross Thou hast redeemed the world.

Priest: Simon of Cyrene was compelled to help Jesus carry His cross, and Jesus accepted his assistance. How willingly would He also permit you to carry the cross: He calls, but you hear not; He invites you, but you decline. What a reproach, to bear the cross reluctantly!

People: O Jesus! Whosoever does not take up his cross and follow Thee, is not worthy of Thee. Behold, I join Thee in the Way of Thy Cross; I will be Thy assistant, following Thy bloody footsteps, that I may come to Thee in eternal life.

Our Father. Hail Mary. Glory Be.

V. Lord Jesus, crucified,
R. Have mercy on us!

All: Is there one who would not weep
Whelmed in miseries so deep
Christ's dear Mother to behold?

Sixth Station

VERONICA WIPES THE FACE OF JESUS

Quis non posset contristari,
Christi Matrem contemplari
Dolentem cum Filio?

SIXTH STATION

VERONICA WIPES THE FACE OF JESUS

V. We adore Thee, O Christ, and we praise Thee,
(*Genuflect*)
R. Because by Thy holy cross Thou hast redeemed the world.

Priest: Veronica, impelled by devotion and compassion, presents her veil to Jesus to wipe His disfigured face. And Jesus imprints on it His holy countenance: a great recompense for so small a service. What return do you make to your Savior for His great and manifold benefits?

People: Most merciful Jesus! What return shall I make for all the benefits Thou hast bestowed upon me? Behold, I consecrate myself entirely to Thy service. I offer and consecrate to Thee my heart: imprint on it Thy sacred image, never again to be effaced by sin.

Our Father. Hail Mary. Glory Be.

V. Lord Jesus, crucified,
R. Have mercy on us!

All: Can the human heart refrain
From partaking in her pain,
In that Mother's pain untold?

Seventh Station

JESUS FALLS THE SECOND TIME

Pro peccatis suae gentis,
Vidit Jesum in tormentis,
Et flagellis subditum.

SEVENTH STATION

JESUS FALLS THE SECOND TIME

V. We adore Thee, O Christ, and we praise Thee, (*Genuflect*)
R. Because by Thy holy cross Thou hast redeemed the world.

Priest: The suffering Jesus, under the weight of His cross, again falls to the ground; but the cruel executioners do not permit Him to rest a moment. Pushing and striking Him, they urge Him onward. It is the frequent repetition of our sins which oppresses Jesus. Witnessing this, how can I continue to sin?

People: O Jesus, Son of David, have mercy on me! Offer me Thy helping hand, and aid me, that I may not fall again into my former sins. From this very moment, I will earnestly strive to reform: nevermore will I sin! Thou, O sole support of the weak, by Thy grace, without which I can do nothing, strengthen me to carry out faithfully this my resolution.

Our Father. Hail Mary. Glory Be.

V. Lord Jesus, crucified,
R. Have mercy on us!

All: Bruised, derided, cursed, defiled,
She beheld her tender child,
All with bloody scourges rent.

Eighth Station

THE WOMEN OF JERUSALEM WEEP OVER JESUS

Vidit suum dulcem natum
Moriendo, desolatum,
Dum emisit spiritum.

EIGHTH STATION

THE WOMEN OF JERUSALEM WEEP OVER JESUS

V. We adore Thee, O Christ, and we praise Thee, (*Genuflect*)
R. Because by Thy holy cross Thou hast redeemed the world.

Priest: These devoted women, moved by compassion, weep over the suffering Savior. But He turns to them, saying: "Weep not for Me, Who am innocent, but weep for yourselves and for your children." Weep thou also, for there is nothing more pleasing to Our Lord and nothing more profitable for thyself, than tears shed from contrition for thy sins.

People: O Jesus, who shall give to my eyes a torrent of tears, that day and night I may weep for my sins? I beseech Thee, through Thy bitter and bloody tears, to move my heart by Thy divine grace, so that from my eyes tears may flow abundantly, and that I may weep all my days over Thy sufferings, and still more over their cause, my sins.

Our Father. Hail Mary. Glory Be.

V. Lord Jesus, crucified,
R. Have mercy on us!

All: For the sins of His own nation
Saw Him hang in desolation
Till His spirit forth He sent.

Ninth Station

JESUS FALLS THE THIRD TIME

Eia Mater, fons amoris,
Me sentire vim doloris.
Fac, ut tecum lugeam.

NINTH STATION

JESUS FALLS THE THIRD TIME

V. We adore Thee, O Christ, and we praise Thee, (*Genuflect*)
R. Because by Thy holy cross Thou hast redeemed the world.

Priest: Jesus, arriving exhausted at the foot of Calvary, falls for the third time to the ground. His love for us, however, is not diminished, not extinguished. What a fearfully oppressive burden our sins must be to cause Jesus to fall so often! Had He, however, not taken them upon Himself, they would have plunged us into the abyss of Hell.

People: Most merciful Jesus, I return Thee infinite thanks for not permitting me to continue in sin and to fall, as I have so often deserved, into the depths of Hell. Enkindle in me an earnest desire of amendment; let me never again relapse, but permit me the grace to persevere in penance to the end of my life.

Our Father. Hail Mary. Glory Be.

V. Lord Jesus, crucified,
R. Have mercy on us!

All: O thou Mother! fount of love,
Touch my spirit from above.
Make my heart with thine accord.

Tenth Station

JESUS IS STRIPPED OF HIS GARMENTS

Fac, ut ardeat cor meum
In amando Christum Deum,
Ut sibi complaceam.

TENTH STATION

JESUS IS STRIPPED OF HIS GARMENTS

V. We adore Thee, O Christ, and we praise Thee, (*Genuflect*)
R. Because by Thy holy cross Thou hast redeemed the world.

Priest: When Our Savior had arrived on Calvary, He was cruelly despoiled of His garments. How painful this must have been because they adhered to His wounded and torn body, and with them parts of His bloody skin were removed! All the wounds of Jesus are torn anew. Jesus was despoiled of His garments that He might die possessed of nothing; how happy will I also die after laying aside my former self with all evil desires and sinful inclinations!

People: Inspire me, O Jesus, to lay aside my former self and to be renewed according to Thy will and desire. I will not spare myself, however painful this should be for me: despoiled of things temporal, of my own will, I desire to die, in order to live for Thee forever.

Our Father. Hail Mary. Glory Be.

V. Lord Jesus, crucified,
R. Have mercy on us!

All: Make me feel as thou hast felt;
Make my soul to glow and melt
With the love of Christ, my Lord.

Eleventh Station

JESUS IS NAILED TO THE CROSS

Sancta Mater istud ages,
Crucifixi fige plagas
Cordi meo valide.

ELEVENTH STATION

JESUS IS NAILED TO THE CROSS

V. We adore Thee, O Christ, and we praise Thee,
(*Genuflect*)
R. Because by Thy holy cross Thou hast redeemed the world.

Priest: Jesus, being stripped of His garments, was violently thrown upon the cross and His hands and feet nailed thereto. In such excruciating pains He remained silent, because it pleased His heavenly Father. He suffered patiently, because He suffered for me. How do I act in sufferings and in troubles? How fretful and impatient, how full of complaints I am!

People: O Jesus, gracious Lamb of God, I renounce forever my impatience. Crucify, O Lord, my flesh and its concupiscences; scourge, scathe, and punish me in this world, do but spare me in the next. I commit my destiny to Thee, resigning myself to Thy holy will: may it be done in all things!

Our Father. Hail Mary. Glory Be.

V. Lord Jesus, crucified,
R. Have mercy on us!

All: Holy Mother, pierce me through!
In my heart each wound renew
Of my Savior crucified.

Twelfth Station

JESUS IS RAISED UPON THE CROSS AND DIES

Tui nati vulnerati,
Tam dignati pro me pati
Poenas mecum divide.

TWELFTH STATION

JESUS IS RAISED UPON THE CROSS AND DIES

V. We adore Thee, O Christ, and we praise Thee,
(*Genuflect*)
R. Because by Thy holy cross Thou hast redeemed the world.

Priest: Behold Jesus crucified! Behold His wounds, received for love of you! His whole appearance betokens love: His head is bent to kiss you; His arms are extended to embrace you; His Heart is open to receive you. O superabundance of love, Jesus, the Son of God, dies upon the cross, that man may live and be delivered from everlasting death!

People: O most amiable Jesus! Who will grant me that I may die for Thee! I will at least endeavor to die to the world. How must I regard the world and its vanities, when I behold Thee hanging on the cross, covered with wounds? O Jesus, receive me into Thy wounded Heart: I belong entirely to Thee; for Thee alone do I desire to live and to die.

Our Father. Hail Mary. Glory Be.

V. Lord Jesus, crucified,
R. Have mercy on us!

All: Let me share with thee His pain,
Who for all our sins was slain,
Who for me in torments died.

Thirteenth Station

JESUS IS TAKEN DOWN FROM THE CROSS AND PLACED IN THE ARMS OF HIS MOTHER

Fac me tecum pie flere,
Crucifixo condolere,
Donec ego vixero.

THIRTEENTH STATION

JESUS IS TAKEN DOWN FROM THE CROSS AND PLACED IN THE ARMS OF HIS MOTHER

V. We adore Thee, O Christ, and we praise Thee, (*Genuflect*)
R. Because by Thy holy cross Thou hast redeemed the world.

Priest: Jesus did not descend from the cross but remained on it until He died. And when taken down from it, He in death as in life, rested on the bosom of His divine Mother. Persevere in your resolutions of reform and do not part from the cross; he who persevereth to the end shall be saved. Consider, moreover, how pure the heart should be that receives the body and blood of Christ in the Adorable Sacrament of the Altar.

People: O Lord Jesus, Thy lifeless body, mangled and lacerated, found a worthy resting-place on the bosom of Thy virgin Mother. Have I not often compelled Thee to dwell in my heart, full of sin and impurity as it was? Create in me a new heart, that I may worthily receive Thy most sacred body in Holy Communion, and that Thou mayest remain in me and I in Thee for all eternity.

Our Father. Hail Mary. Glory Be.

V. Lord Jesus, crucified,
R. Have mercy on us!

All: Let me mingle tears with thee,
Mourning Him Who mourned for me,
All the days that I may live.

Fourteenth Station

JESUS IS LAID IN THE SEPULCHRE

Juxta crucem tecum stare,
Et me tibi sociare,
In planctu desidero.

FOURTEENTH STATION

JESUS IS LAID IN THE SEPULCHRE

V. We adore Thee, O Christ, and we praise Thee,
(*Genuflect*)
R. Because by Thy holy cross Thou hast redeemed the world.

Priest: The body of Jesus is interred in a stranger's sepulchre. He who in this world had not whereupon to rest His head, would not even have a grave of His own, because He was not from this world. You, who are so attached to the world, henceforth despise it, that you may not perish with it.

People: O Jesus, Thou hast set me apart from the world; what, then, shall I seek therein? Thou hast created me for Heaven; what, then, have I to do with the world? Depart from me, deceitful world, with thy vanities! Henceforth I will follow the Way of the Cross traced out for me by my Redeemer, and journey onward to my heavenly home, there to dwell forever and ever.

Our Father. Hail Mary. Glory Be.

V. Lord Jesus, crucified,
R. Have mercy on us!

All: By the cross with thee to stay,
There with thee to weep and pray,
Is all I ask of thee to give.

CONCLUDING PRAYER

Together: Almighty and eternal God, merciful Father, who hast given to the human race Thy beloved Son as an example of humility, obedience, and patience, to precede us on the way of life, bearing the cross: Graciously grant us that we, inflamed by His infinite love, may take up the sweet yoke of His Gospel, together with the mortification of the cross, following Him as His true disciples, so that we shall one day gloriously rise with Him and joyfully hear the final sentence: "Come, ye blessed of My Father, and possess the kingdom which was prepared for you from the beginning," where Thou reignest with the Son and the Holy Ghost, and where we hope to reign with Thee, world without end. *Amen.*

STABAT MATER

(Concluding Hymn)

Virgo virginum praeclara, *Mihi jam non sis amara,* *Fac me tecum plangere;*	*Virgin of all virgins best!* *Listen to my fond request:* *Let me share thy grief divine;*
Fac, ut portem Christi mortem, *Passionis fac consortem,* *Et plagas recolere.*	*Let me, to my latest breath,* *In my body bear the death* *Of that dying Son of thine.*
Fac me plagis vulnerari, *Fac me cruce inebriari,* *Et cruore Filii.*	*Wounded with His every wound,* *Steep my soul till it hath swooned* *In His very Blood away.*
Flammis ne urar succensus *Per te, Virgo, sim defensus* *In die judicii.*	*Be to me, O Virgin, nigh,* *Lest in flames I burn and die,* *In His awful Judgment Day.*
Christe, cum sit hinc exire, *Da per Matrem me venire* *Ad palman victoriae*	*Christ, when Thou shalt* *call me hence,* *Be Thy Mother my defense,* *Be Thy cross my victory.*
Quando corpus morietur, *Fac ut animae donetur* *Paradisi gloria.* *Amen.*	*While my body here decays,* *May my soul Thy goodness praise,* *Safe in paradise with Thee.* *Amen.*
V. Ora pro nobis, Virgo *dolorosissima.* **R.** *Ut digni efficiamur promis-* *sionibus Christi.*	*V. Pray for us, Virgin most* *sorrowful.* **R.** *That we may be made worthy* *of the promises of Christ.*

OREMUS

Interveniat pro nobis, quaesumus, Domine Jesu Christe, nunc et in hora mortis nostrae, apud tuam clementiam, beata Virgo Maria Mater tua, cujus sacratissimam animam in hora tuae passionis doloris gladius pertransivit. Per te, Jesu Christe, salvator mundi, qui cum Patre et Spiritu Sancto vivis et regnas, per omnia saecula saeculorum. *Amen.*

LET US PRAY

Grant, we beseech Thee, O Lord Jesus Christ, that the most blessed Virgin Mary, Thy Mother, through whose most holy soul, in the hour of Thine own Passion, the sword of sorrow passed, may intercede for us before the throne of Thy mercy, now and at the hour of our death. Through Thee, Jesus Christ, Savior of the world, Who livest and reignest with the Father and the Holy Ghost, now and forever. *Amen.*

NOTE: How to gain partial or plenary indulgence, see page 179.

THE WAY OF THE CROSS

According to the Method of

ST. ALPHONSUS LIGUORI

Let each one, kneeling before the high altar, make an Act of Contrition, and form the intention of gaining the indulgences connected to this devotion, whether for himself or for the souls in Purgatory.

ACT OF CONTRITION MY GOD

O, my God, I am heartily sorry for having offended Thee, and I detest all my sins because of Thy just punishments, but most of all because they offend Thee, my God, Who art all-good and deserving of all my love. I firmly resolve, with the help of Thy grace, to sin no more and to avoid the near occasions of sin. *Amen.*

Following the Act of Contrition, all say:

PREPARATORY PRAYER

All: My Lord Jesus Christ, Thou hast made this journey to die for me with love unutterable, and I have so many times unworthily abandoned Thee; but now I love Thee with my whole heart, and because I love Thee, I repent sincerely for having ever offended Thee. Pardon me, my God, and permit me to accompany Thee on this journey. Thou goest to die for love of me; I wish also, my beloved Redeemer, to die for love of Thee. My Jesus, I will live and die always united to Thee. *Amen.*

First Station

JESUS IS CONDEMNED TO DEATH

Stabat Mater dolorosa,
Juxta crucem lacrymosa,
Dum pendebat Filius.

FIRST STATION

JESUS IS CONDEMNED TO DEATH

V. We adore Thee, O Christ, and we praise Thee, (*Genuflect*)
R. Because by Thy holy cross Thou hast redeemed the world.

Priest: Consider that Jesus, after having been scourged and crowned with thorns, was unjustly condemned by Pilate to die on the cross.

All: My adorable Jesus, it was not Pilate, no, it was my sins, that condemned Thee to die. I beseech Thee, by the merits of this sorrowful journey, to assist my soul in its journey toward eternity. I love Thee, my beloved Jesus; I love Thee more than myself; I repent with my whole heart of having offended Thee. Never permit me to separate myself from Thee again. Grant that I may love Thee always, and then do with me what Thou wilt.

Our Father. Hail Mary. Glory Be.

All: At the cross her station keeping,
Stood the mournful Mother weeping,
Close to Jesus to the last.

Second Station

JESUS IS MADE TO CARRY HIS CROSS

Cujus animam gementem,
Contristatam et dolentem,
Pertransivit gladius.

SECOND STATION

JESUS IS MADE TO CARRY HIS CROSS

V. We adore Thee, O Christ, and we praise Thee, (*Genuflect*)
R. Because by Thy holy cross Thou hast redeemed the world.

Priest: Consider that Jesus, in making this journey with the cross on His shoulders, thought of us and offered for us to His Father the death that He was about to undergo.

People: My most beloved Jesus, I embrace all the tribulations that Thou hast destined for me until death. I beseech Thee, by the merits of the pain Thou didst suffer in carrying Thy cross, to give me the necessary help to carry mine with perfect patience and resignation. I love Thee, Jesus, my love; I repent of having offended Thee. Never permit me to separate myself from Thee again. Grant that I may love Thee always, and then do with me what Thou wilt.

Our Father. Hail Mary. Glory Be.

All: Through her heart, His sorrow sharing,
All His bitter anguish bearing,
Now at length the sword has passed.

Third Station

JESUS FALLS THE FIRST TIME

O quam tristis et afflicta
Fuit illa benedicta
Mater Unigeniti!

THIRD STATION

JESUS FALLS THE FIRST TIME

V. We adore Thee, O Christ, and we praise Thee, (*Genuflect*)
R. Because by Thy holy cross Thou hast redeemed the world.

Priest: Consider this first fall of Jesus under His cross. His flesh was torn by the scourges, His head crowned with thorns, and He had lost a great quantity of blood. He was so weakened that He could scarcely walk, and yet He had to carry this great load upon His shoulders. The soldiers struck Him rudely, and thus He fell several times in His journey.

People: My beloved Jesus, it is not the weight of the cross, but of my sins, which has made Thee suffer so much pain. Ah, by the merits of this first fall, deliver me from the misfortune of falling into mortal sin. I love Thee, O my Jesus, with my whole heart; I repent of having offended Thee. Never permit me to offend Thee again. Grant that I may love Thee always; and then do with me what Thou wilt.

Our Father. Hail Mary. Glory Be.

All: O, how sad and sore distressed
Was that Mother highly blessed
Of the sole-begotten One!

Fourth Station

JESUS MEETS HIS SORROWFUL MOTHER

Quae moerebat, et dolebat,
Pia Mater dum videbat
Nati poenas inclyti.

FOURTH STATION

JESUS MEETS HIS SORROWFUL MOTHER

V. We adore Thee, O Christ, and we praise Thee, (*Genuflect*)
R. Because by Thy holy cross Thou hast redeemed the world.

Priest: Consider the meeting of the Son and the Mother, which took place on this journey. Jesus and Mary looked at each other, and their looks became as so many arrows to wound those hearts which loved each other so tenderly.

People: My most loving Jesus, by the sorrow Thou didst experience in this meeting, grant me the grace of a truly devoted love for Thy most holy Mother. And thou, my Queen, who was overwhelmed with sorrow, obtain for me by thy intercession a continual and tender remembrance of the Passion of thy Son. I love Thee, Jesus, my love; I repent of ever having offended Thee. Never permit me to offend Thee again. Grant that I may love Thee always; and then do with me what Thou wilt.

Our Father. Hail Mary. Glory Be.

All: Christ above in torment hangs,
She beneath beholds the pangs
Of her dying, glorious Son.

Fifth Station

SIMON OF CYRENE HELPS JESUS TO CARRY HIS CROSS

Quis est homo qui non fleret
Matrem Christi si videret
In tanto supplicio?

FIFTH STATION

SIMON OF CYRENE HELPS JESUS TO CARRY HIS CROSS

V. We adore Thee, O Christ, and we praise Thee,
(*Genuflect*)
R. Because by Thy holy cross Thou hast redeemed the world.

Priest: Consider how weak and weary Jesus was. At each step He was at the point of expiring. Fearing that He would die on the way when they wished Him to die the infamous death of the cross, they forced Simon of Cyrene to help carry the cross after Our Lord.

People: My most sweet Jesus, I will not refuse the cross as the Cyrenian did; I accept it, I embrace it. I accept in particular the death that Thou hast destined for me, with all the pains which may accompany it. I unite it to Thy death; I offer it to Thee. Thou hast died for love of me! I will die for love of Thee, and to please Thee. Help me by Thy grace. I love Thee, Jesus, my love; I repent of having offended Thee. Never permit me to offend Thee again. Grant that I may love Thee always; and then do with me what Thou wilt.

Our Father. Hail Mary. Glory Be.

All: Is there one who would not weep
Whelmed in miseries so deep
Christ's dear Mother to behold?

Sixth Station

VERONICA WIPES THE FACE OF JESUS

Quis non posset contristari,
Christi Matrem contemplari
Dolentem cum Filio?

SIXTH STATION

VERONICA WIPES THE FACE OF JESUS

V. We adore Thee, O Christ, and we praise Thee,
(*Genuflect*)
R. Because by Thy holy cross Thou hast redeemed the world.

Priest: Consider that the holy woman named Veronica, seeing Jesus so afflicted and His face bathed in sweat and blood, presented Him with a towel, with which He wiped His adorable face, leaving on it the impression of His holy countenance.

People: My most beloved Jesus. Thy face was beautiful before, but in this journey it has lost all its beauty, and wounds and blood have disfigured it. Alas! my soul also was once beautiful, when it received Thy grace in Baptism, but I have disfigured it since by my sins. Thou alone, my Redeemer, canst restore it to its former beauty. Do this by Thy Passion, O Jesus. I repent of having offended Thee. Never permit me to offend Thee again. Grant that I may love Thee always; and then do with me what Thou wilt.

Our Father. Hail Mary. Glory Be.

All: Can the human heart refrain
From partaking in her pain,
In that Mother's pain untold?

Seventh Station

JESUS FALLS THE SECOND TIME

Pro peccatis suae gentis,
Vidit Jesum in tormentis,
Et flagellis subditum.

SEVENTH STATION
JESUS FALLS THE SECOND TIME

V. We adore Thee, O Christ, and we praise Thee,
(*Genuflect*)
R. Because by Thy holy cross Thou hast redeemed the world.

Priest: Consider the second fall of Jesus under the cross—a fall which renews the pains of all the wounds of the head and members of our afflicted Lord.

People: My most gentle Jesus, how many times Thou hast pardoned me, and how many times have I fallen again, and begun again to offend Thee! O, by the merits of this new fall, give me the necessary help to persevere in Thy grace until death. Grant that in all temptations which assail me I may always commend myself to Thee. I love Thee, Jesus, my love, with my whole heart; I repent of having offended Thee. Never permit me to offend Thee again. Grant that I may love Thee always; and then do with me what Thou wilt.

Our Father. Hail Mary. Glory Be.

All: Bruised, derided, cursed, defiled,
She beheld her tender child,
All with bloody scourges rent.

Eighth Station

THE WOMEN OF JERUSALEM WEEP OVER JESUS

Vidit suum dulcem natum
Moriendo, desolatum,
Dum emisit spiritum.

EIGHTH STATION

THE WOMEN OF JERUSALEM WEEP OVER JESUS

V. We adore Thee, O Christ, and we praise Thee,
(*Genuflect*)
R. Because by Thy holy cross Thou hast redeemed the world.

Priest: Consider that those women wept with compassion at seeing Jesus in so pitiable a state, streaming with blood, as He walked along. But Jesus said to them, "Weep not for Me, but for your children."

People: My Jesus, laden with sorrows, I weep for the offences that I have committed against Thee, because of the pains which they have deserved, and still more because of the displeasure which they have caused Thee, Who hast loved me so much. It is Thy love, more than the fear of Hell, which causes me to weep for my sins. My Jesus, I love Thee more than myself; I repent of having offended Thee. Never permit me to offend Thee again. Grant that I may love Thee always; and then do with me what Thou wilt.

Our Father. Hail Mary. Glory Be.

All: For the sins of His own nation
Saw Him hang in desolation
Till His spirit forth He sent.

Ninth Station

JESUS FALLS THE THIRD TIME

Eia Mater, fons amoris,
Me sentire vim doloris.
Fac, ut tecum lugeam.

NINTH STATION

JESUS FALLS THE THIRD TIME

V. We adore Thee, O Christ, and we praise Thee,
(*Genuflect*)
R. Because by Thy holy cross Thou hast redeemed the world.

Priest: Consider the third fall of Jesus Christ. His weakness was extreme, and the cruelty of His executioners excessive, who tried to hasten His steps when He had scarcely strength to move.

People: Ah, my outraged Jesus, by the merits of the weakness that Thou didst suffer in going to Calvary, give me strength sufficient to conquer all human respect and all my wicked passions, which have led me to despise Thy friendship. I love Thee, Jesus, my love, with my whole heart; I repent of having offended Thee. Never permit me to offend Thee again. Grant that I may love Thee always; and then do with me what Thou wilt.

Our Father. Hail Mary. Glory Be.

All: O thou Mother! fount of love,
Touch my spirit from above.
Make my heart with thine accord.

Tenth Station

JESUS IS STRIPPED OF HIS GARMENTS

Fac, ut ardeat cor meum
In amando Christum Deum,
Ut sibi complaceam.

TENTH STATION

JESUS IS STRIPPED OF HIS GARMENTS

V. We adore Thee, O Christ, and we praise Thee, (*Genuflect*)

R. Because by Thy holy cross Thou hast redeemed the world.

Priest: Consider the violence with which the executioners stripped Jesus. His inner garments adhered to His torn flesh, and they dragged them off so roughly that the skin came with them. Compassionate your Savior thus cruelly treated, and say to Him:

People: My innocent Jesus, by the merits of the torment which Thou hast felt, help me to strip myself of all affection to things of earth, in order that I may place all my love in Thee, Who art so worthy of my love. I love Thee, O Jesus, with my whole heart; I repent of having offended Thee. Never permit me to offend Thee again. Grant that I may love Thee always; and then do with me what Thou wilt.

Our Father. Hail Mary. Glory Be.

All: Make me feel as thou hast felt;
Make my soul to glow and melt
With the love of Christ, my Lord.

Eleventh Station

JESUS IS NAILED TO THE CROSS

Sancta Mater istud ages,
Crucifixi fige plagas
Cordi meo valide.

ELEVENTH STATION

JESUS IS NAILED TO THE CROSS

V. We adore Thee, O Christ, and we praise Thee, *(Genuflect)*
R. Because by Thy holy cross Thou hast redeemed the world.

Priest: Consider that Jesus, after being thrown on the cross, extended His hands, and offered to His eternal Father the sacrifice of His life for our salvation. These barbarians fastened Him with nails, and then, raising the cross, left Him to die with anguish on this infamous gibbet.

People: My Jesus, loaded with contempt, nail my heart to Thy feet, that it may ever remain there to love Thee and never quit Thee again. I love Thee more than myself; I repent of having offended Thee. Never permit me to offend Thee again. Grant that I may love Thee always; and then do with me what Thou wilt.

Our Father. Hail Mary. Glory Be.

All: Holy Mother, pierce me through!
In my heart each wound renew
Of my Savior crucified.

Twelfth Station

JESUS IS RAISED UPON THE CROSS AND DIES

Tui nati vulnerati,
Tam dignati pro me pati
Poenas mecum divide.

TWELFTH STATION

JESUS IS RAISED UPON THE CROSS AND DIES

V. We adore Thee, O Christ, and we praise Thee,
(Genuflect)
R. Because by Thy holy cross Thou hast redeemed the world.

Priest: Consider how thy Jesus, after three hours of agony on the cross, consumed at length with anguish, abandons Himself to the weight of His body, bows His head, and dies.

People: O my dying Jesus, I kiss devoutly the cross on which Thou didst die for love of me. I have merited by my sins to die a miserable death, but Thy death is my hope. Ah, by the merits of Thy death, give me grace to die, embracing Thy feet and burning with love for Thee. I commit my soul into Thy hands. I love Thee with my whole heart; I repent of ever having offended Thee. Never permit me to offend Thee again. Grant that I may love Thee always; and then do with me what Thou wilt.

Our Father. Hail Mary. Glory Be.

All: Let me share with thee His pain,
Who for all our sins was slain.
Who for me in torments died.

Thirteenth Station

JESUS IS TAKEN DOWN FROM THE CROSS AND PLACED IN THE ARMS OF HIS MOTHER

Fac me tecum pie flere,
Crucifixo condolere,
Donec ego vixero.

THIRTEENTH STATION

JESUS IS TAKEN DOWN FROM THE CROSS AND PLACED IN THE ARMS OF HIS MOTHER

V. We adore Thee, O Christ, and we praise Thee, (*Genuflect*)
R. Because by Thy holy cross Thou hast redeemed the world.

Priest: Consider that Our Lord having expired, two of His disciples, Joseph and Nicodemus, took Him down from the cross and placed Him in the arms of His afflicted Mother, who received Him with unutterable tenderness and pressed Him to her bosom.

People: O Mother of Sorrow, for the love of this Son, accept me for thy servant, and pray to Him for me. And Thou, my Redeemer, since Thou hast died for me, permit me to love Thee; for I wish but Thee, my Jesus, and I repent of ever having offended Thee. Never permit me to offend Thee again. Grant that I may love Thee always; and then do with me what Thou wilt.

Our Father. Hail Mary. Glory Be.

All: Let me mingle tears with thee,
Mourning Him Who mourned for me,
All the days that I may live.

Fourteenth Station

JESUS IS LAID IN THE SEPULCHRE

Juxta crucem tecum stare,
Et me tibi sociare,
In planctu desidero.

FOURTEENTH STATION

JESUS IS LAID IN THE SEPULCHRE

V. We adore Thee, O Christ, and we praise Thee, (*Genuflect*)
R. Because by Thy holy cross Thou hast redeemed the world.

Priest: Consider that the disciples carried the body of Jesus to bury it, accompanied by His holy Mother, who arranged it in the sepulchre with her own hands. They then closed the tomb, and all withdrew.

People: Ah, my buried Jesus, I kiss the stone that encloses Thee. But Thou didst rise again the third day. I beseech Thee, by Thy resurrection, make me rise glorious with Thee at the Last Day, to be always united with Thee in Heaven, to praise Thee and love Thee forever. I love Thee, and I repent of ever having offended Thee. Never permit me to offend Thee again. Grant that I may love Thee always; and then do with me what Thou wilt.

Our Father. Hail Mary. Glory Be.

All: By the cross with Thee to stay,
There with Thee to weep and pray,
Is all I ask of Thee to give.

CONCLUDING PRAYERS

After this, return to the high altar and, to complete the devotion, say the *Our Father, Hail Mary*, and *Glory Be* five times in honor of the Passion of Jesus Christ.

PRAYER TO JESUS CRUCIFIED

Behold, O kind and most sweet Jesus, I cast myself upon my knees in Thy sight, and with the most fervent desire of my soul, I pray and beseech Thee that Thou wouldst impress upon my heart lively sentiments of faith, hope, and charity, with true contrition for my sins and a firm purpose of amendment; while with deep affection and grief of soul, I ponder within myself and mentally contemplate Thy five wounds, having before my eyes the words which David the prophet put on Thy lips concerning Thee: "They have pierced My hands and My feet, they have numbered all My bones."

At the end, one Our Father and Hail Mary, at least, should be said for the intention of the Sovereign Pontiff; this will fulfill the requirements for a plenary indulgence connected to this devotion—so long as a person also fulfills the other requirements. (NOTE: See page 179 for a full explanation of how to gain a plenary indulgence by making this devotion.)

STABAT MATER

(Conclusion Hymn)

Virgo virginum praeclara, Mihi jam non sis amara, Fac me tecum plangere;	*Virgin of all virgins best! Listen to my fond request: Let me share thy grief divine;*
Fac, ut portem Christi mortem, Passionis fac consortem, Et plagas recolere.	*Let me, to my latest breath, In my body bear the death Of that dying Son of thine.*
Fac me plagis vulnerari, Fac me cruce inebriari, Et cruore Filii.	*Wounded with His every wound, Steep my soul till it hath swooned In His very Blood away.*
Flammis ne urar succensus Per te, Virgo, sim defensus In die judicii.	*Be to me, O Virgin, nigh, Lest in flames I burn and die, In His awful Judgment Day.*
Christe, cum sit hinc exire, Da per Matrem me venire Ad palman victoriae	*Christ, when Thou shalt call me hence, Be Thy Mother my defense, Be Thy cross my victory.*
Quando corpus morietur, Fac ut animae donetur Paradisi gloria. Amen.	*While my body here decays, May my soul Thy goodness praise, Safe in paradise with Thee. Amen.*
V. Ora pro nobis, Virgo dolorosissima.	*V. Pray for us, Virgin most sorrowful.*
R. *Ut digni efficiamur promissionibus Christi.*	**R.** *That we may be made worthy of the promises of Christ.*

OREMUS

Interveniat pro nobis, quaesumus, Domine Jesu Christe, nunc et in hora mortis nostrae, apud tuam clementiam, beata Virgo Maria Mater tua, cujus sacratissimam animam in hora tuae passionis doloris gladius pertransivit. Per te, Jesu Christe, salvator mundi, qui cum Patre et Spiritu Sancto vivis et regnas, per omnia saecula saeculorum. *Amen.*

LET US PRAY

Grant, we beseech Thee, O Lord Jesus Christ, that the most blessed Virgin Mary, Thy Mother, through whose most holy soul, in the hour of Thine own Passion, the sword of sorrow passed, may intercede for us before the throne of Thy mercy, now and at the hour of our death. Through Thee, Jesus Christ, Saviour of the world, Who livest and reignest with the Father and the Holy Ghost, now and forever. *Amen.*

WAY OF THE CROSS

According to the Method of

ST. JOHN HENRY CARDINAL NEWMAN

ACT OF CONTRITION

O my God, I am heartily sorry for having offended Thee, and I detest all my sins because of Thy just punishments, but most of all because they offend Thee, my God, Who art all-good and deserving of all my love. I firmly resolve, with the help of Thy grace, to sin no more and to avoid the near occasions of sin.

OUR FATHER

Our Father, Who art in Heaven, hallowed be Thy name; Thy Kingdom come, Thy will be done on earth as it is in Heaven. Give us this day our daily bread; and forgive us our trespasses as we forgive those who trespass against us; and lead us not into temptation, but deliver us from evil. Amen.

HAIL MARY

Hail Mary, full of Grace, the Lord is with thee. Blessed art thou among women and blessed is the fruit of thy womb Jesus. Holy Mary, Mother of God, pray for us sinners now and at the hour of our death. Amen.

GLORY BE

Glory be to the Father, to the Son, and to the Holy Spirit. As it was in the beginning, is now and ever shall be, world without end. Amen.

PRAYER BEFORE THE CRUCIFIX

Look down upon me, good and gentle Jesus while before Your face I humbly kneel and, with burning soul, pray and beseech You to fix deep in my heart lively sentiments of faith, hope, and charity; true contrition for my sins, and a firm purpose of amendment. While I contemplate, with great love and tender pity, Your five most precious wounds, pondering over them within me and calling to mind the words which David, Your prophet, said to You, my Jesus: "They have pierced My hands and My feet, they have numbered all My bones." Amen.

The First Station

JESUS IS CONDEMNED TO DEATH

V. Adoramus te, Christe, et benedicimus tibi.
R. Quia per sanctam Crucem tuam redemisti mundum.

V. We adore Thee O Christ and we praise Thee. (*Genuflect*)
R. Because by Thy Holy Cross Thou hast redeemed the world.

Jesus was taken from the House of Caiaphas, only to be dragged before Pilate and Herod. Again, He was mocked, beaten, and spit upon, and His back torn with scourges, His head crowned with thorns. Jesus, who on the last day will judge the world, is Himself condemned by unjust judges to a death of ignominy and torture.

Jesus is condemned to death. His death-warrant is signed, and who signed it? I did, when I committed my first mortal sins! My first mortal sins, when I fell away from the state of grace that You placed me in at my baptism. These were truly Your death-warrant, O Lord! The Innocent suffered for the guilty. Those sins of mine were the voices which cried out, "Let Him be crucified." The very willingness and delight in my heart when I committed them was the consent which Pilate gave to this unruly mob. The blows and the blasphemies with which the fierce soldiers and the populace received You, these were none other than the hardness of heart which followed my sins, as well as my disgust, my despair, my proud impatience, my obstinate resolve to continue sinning, and the love of sin which took possession of me. What were these contrary and impetuous feelings, but the executioners carrying out the sentence which Pilate had pronounced?

Our Father, Hail Mary, Glory Be.

V. Have Mercy upon us O Lord.
R. Have Mercy on us.

May the souls of the faithful departed, through the mercy of God, rest in peace.

The Second Station

JESUS RECEIVES HIS CROSS

V. Adoramus te, Christe, et benedicimus tibi.
R. Quia per sanctam Crucem tuam redemisti mundum.

V. We adore Thee O Christ and we praise Thee. (*Genuflect*)
R. Because by Thy Holy Cross Thou hast redeemed the world.

A strong (and thus heavy) Cross is placed upon His torn shoulders. It is stout enough to hold Him on it when

He arrives at Calvary. Nevertheless, He does not merely receive it with gentleness and meekness, but also with gladness of heart, for it is to be the salvation of mankind.

At the same time, remember that this heavy Cross is the weight of our sins. As it fell upon His neck and shoulders, it came down with a shock. Alas! what a sudden, heavy weight have I laid upon You, O Jesus. And, though in the calm and clear foresight of Your mind—for You see all things—You were fully prepared for it, yet Your weakened frame tottered under it when it dropped upon You. How great a misery is it that I have lifted up my hand against my God. How could I ever think that He would forgive me! Unless He had Himself told us that He underwent His bitter passion so as to forgive us. I acknowledge, O Jesus, in the anguish and agony of my heart, that it was my sins that struck You on the face, that bruised Your sacred arms, that tore Your flesh with iron rods, that nailed You to the Cross, and let You slowly die upon it.

Our Father, Hail Mary, Glory Be.

V. Have Mercy upon us O Lord.
R. Have Mercy on us.

May the souls of the faithful departed, through the mercy of God, rest in peace.

The Third Station

JESUS FALLS THE FIRST TIME BENEATH THE CROSS

V. Adoramus te, Christe, et benedicimus tibi.
R. Quia per sanctam Crucem tuam redemisti mundum.

V. We adore Thee O Christ and we praise Thee. (*Genuflect*)
R. Because by Thy Holy Cross Thou hast redeemed the world.

Jesus, bowed down under the weight and the length of the unwieldy Cross, slowly sets forth on His way, amid the mockeries and insults of the crowd. His agony in the Garden itself was enough to exhaust Him! Yet, it was only the first of many sufferings. He sets off with His whole heart, but His limbs fail Him, and He falls.

Yes, it is as I feared. Jesus, the strong and mighty Lord, has found for the moment our sins stronger than Himself. He falls—yet He bore the load for a while; He tottered, but He bore up and walked onwards. What, then, made Him give way? I say, I repeat, it is an intimation and a memory to you, O my soul, of your falling back into mortal sin. I repented of the sins of my youth and went on well for a time; but at length a new temptation came, when I was off my guard, and I suddenly fell away. Then all my good habits seemed to go at once; they were like a garment which is stripped off, so quickly and utterly did grace depart from me. And at that moment I looked at my Lord, and lo! He had fallen down, and I covered my face with my hands and remained in a state of great confusion.

Our Father, Hail Mary, Glory Be.

V. Have Mercy upon us O Lord.
R. Have Mercy on us.

May the souls of the faithful departed, through the mercy of God, rest in peace.

The Fourth Station

JESUS MEETS HIS MOTHER

V. Adoramus te, Christe, et benedicimus tibi.
R. Quia per sanctam Crucem tuam redemisti mundum.

V. We adore Thee O Christ and we praise Thee. (*Genuflect*)
R. Because by Thy Holy Cross Thou hast redeemed the world.

Jesus rises, though wounded by His fall, journeys on, with His Cross still on His shoulders. He is bent down;

but at one place, looking up, He sees His Mother. For an instant they just see each other, and He goes forward.

Mary would rather have had all His sufferings herself, could that have been, than not have known what they were by being away from Him. He, too, gained a refreshment, as from some soothing and grateful breath of air, to see her sad smile amid the sights and the noises which were about Him. She had known Him beautiful and glorious, with the freshness of Divine Innocence and peace upon His countenance. *Now* she saw Him so changed and deformed that she could hardly recognize Him, save for the piercing, thrilling, peace-inspiring look He gave her. Still, He was now carrying the load of the world's sins, and, all-holy though He was, He carried the image of them on His very face; He looked like some outcast or outlaw who had frightful guilt upon Him. He that knew no sin became sin for us; He knew not its form, not a limb, but spoke of guilt, of a curse, of punishment, of agony.

What a meeting of Son and Mother! Yet there was a mutual comfort, for there was a mutual sympathy. Jesus and Mary—do they forget that Passion-tide through all eternity?

Our Father, Hail Mary, Glory Be.

V. Have Mercy upon us O Lord.
R. Have Mercy on us.

May the souls of the faithful departed, through the mercy of God, rest in peace.

The Fifth Station

SIMON OF CYRENE HELPS JESUS TO CARRY THE CROSS

V. Adoramus te, Christe, et benedicimus tibi.
R. Quia per sanctam Crucem tuam redemisti mundum.

V. We adore Thee O Christ and we praise Thee. (*Genuflect*)
R. Because by Thy Holy Cross Thou hast redeemed the world.

At length His strength utterly fails, and He is unable to proceed. The executioners stand perplexed. What are they to do? How is He to get to Calvary? Soon they see a stranger who seems strong and active—Simon of Cyrene. They seize on him and compel him to carry the Cross with Jesus. The sight of the Sufferer pierces the man's heart. Oh, what a privilege! O happy soul, elect of God! he takes the part assigned to him with joy.

This came of Mary's intercession. *He* prayed, not for Himself, except that He might drink the full chalice of suffering and do His Father's will; but *she* showed herself a mother by following Him with her prayers, since she could help Him in no other way. She then sent this stranger to help Him. It was she who led the soldiers to see that they might be too fierce with Him. Sweet Mother, even *do* the like to us. Pray for us ever, Holy Mother of God, pray for us, whatever be our cross, as we pass along on our way. Pray for us, and we shall rise again, though we have fallen. Pray for us when sorrow, anxiety, or sickness comes upon us. Pray for us when we are prostrate under the power of temptation, and send some faithful servant of yours to hold us up. And in the world to come, if found worthy to expiate our sins in the fiery prison, send some good Angel to give us a period of refreshment. Pray for us, Holy Mother of God.

Our Father, Hail Mary, Glory Be.

V. Have Mercy upon us O Lord.
R. Have Mercy on us.

May the souls of the faithful departed, through the mercy of God, rest in peace.

The Sixth Station

JESUS AND VERONICA

V. Adoramus te, Christe, et benedicimus tibi.
R. Quia per sanctam Crucem tuam redemisti mundum.

V. We adore Thee O Christ and we praise Thee. (*Genuflect*)
R. Because by Thy Holy Cross Thou hast redeemed the world.

As Jesus toils along up the hill, covered with the sweat of death, a woman makes her way through the crowd, and wipes His face with a napkin. In reward for her piety the cloth retains the impression of the Sacred Face upon it.

The relief which a Mother's tenderness secured is not yet all she did. Her prayers sent Veronica as well as Simon—Simon to do a man's work, Veronica to do the part of a woman. The devout servant of Jesus did what she could. As Magdalen had poured the ointment at the Feast, so Veronica now offered Him this napkin in His passion. "Ah," she said, "would that I could do more! Why have I not the strength of Simon, to take part in the burden of the Cross? But men only can serve the Great High Priest, now that He is celebrating the solemn act of sacrifice." O Jesus! let us one and all minister to You according to our places and powers. And as You accepted refreshment from Your followers during Your hour of trial, so give to us the support of Your grace when we are hard pressed by our foe. I feel I cannot bear up against temptation, weariness, despondency, and sin. I say to myself, what is the good of being religious? I shall fall, O my dear Savior, I shall certainly fall, unless You will renew for me my vigor like the eagle's and breathe life into me by the soothing application and the touch of the Holy Sacraments which You have appointed.

Our Father, Hail Mary, Glory Be.

V. Have Mercy upon us O Lord.
R. Have Mercy on us.

May the souls of the faithful departed, through the mercy of God, rest in peace.

The Seventh Station

JESUS FALLS THE SECOND TIME

V. Adoramus te, Christe, et benedicimus tibi.
R. Quia per sanctam Crucem tuam redemisti mundum.

V. We adore Thee O Christ and we praise Thee. (*Genuflect*)
R. Because by Thy Holy Cross Thou hast redeemed the world.

The pain of His wounds, and the loss of blood increasing at every step of His way, again His limbs fail Him, and He falls on the ground.

What has He done to deserve all this? This is the reward received by the long-expected Messiah from the Chosen People, the Children of Israel. I know what to answer. He falls because I have fallen. I have fallen again. I know well that, without Your grace, O Lord, I could not stand; and I fancied that I had kept closely to Your Sacraments! Yet, in spite of my going to Mass and to my duties, I am out of grace again. Why is it, except that I have lost my devotional spirit, and have come to Your holy ordinances in a cold, formal way, without inward affection. I became lukewarm, tepid. I thought the battle of life was over and became secure. I had no lively faith, no sight of spiritual things. I came to church from habit, and because I thought others would observe it. I ought to be a new creature, I ought to live by faith, hope, and charity. Instead, I thought more of this world than of the world to come—and at last I forgot that I was a servant of God, and followed the broad way that leads to destruction, not the narrow way which leads to life. And thus, I fell from You.

Our Father, Hail Mary, Glory Be.

V. Have Mercy upon us O Lord.
R. Have Mercy on us.

May the souls of the faithful departed, through the mercy of God, rest in peace.

The Eighth Station

JESUS COMFORTS THE WOMEN OF JERUSALEM

V. Adoramus te, Christe, et benedicimus tibi.
R. Quia per sanctam Crucem tuam redemisti mundum.

V. We adore Thee O Christ and we praise Thee. (*Genuflect*)
R. Because by Thy Holy Cross Thou hast redeemed the world.

At the sight of the sufferings of Jesus, the Holy Women are so pierced with grief that they cry out and bewail

Him, careless what happens to them by so doing. Jesus, turning to them, said, "Daughters of Jerusalem, weep not over Me, but weep for yourselves and for your children."

Could it be, O Lord, that I shall prove one of those sinful children for whom You command their mothers to weep? "Weep not for Me," He said, "for I am the Lamb of God, and am making atonement at My own will for the sins of the world. I am suffering now, but I shall triumph!

When I triumph, those souls, for whom I am dying, will either be my dearest friends or my deadliest enemies." Is it possible? O my Lord, can I grasp the terrible thought that You really did weep for me—weep for me, as You wept over Jerusalem? Is it possible that I am one of the reprobate? possible that I shall lose by Your passion and death, not gain by it? O, withdraw not from me. I am in a very bad way. I have so much evil in me. I have so little of an earnest, brave spirit to set against that evil. O Lord, what will become of me? It is so difficult for me to drive away the Evil Spirit from my heart. You alone can completely cast him out.

Our Father, Hail Mary, Glory Be.

V. Have Mercy upon us O Lord.
R. Have Mercy on us.

May the souls of the faithful departed, through the mercy of God, rest in peace.

The Ninth Station

JESUS FALLS THE THIRD TIME

V. Adoramus te, Christe, et benedicimus tibi.
R. Quia per sanctam Crucem tuam redemisti mundum.

V. We adore Thee O Christ and we praise Thee. (*Genuflect*)
R. Because by Thy Holy Cross Thou hast redeemed the world.

Jesus had now reached almost to the top of Calvary; but, before He had gained the very spot where He was to be crucified, again He fell and is again dragged up and goaded onwards by the brutal soldiery.

We are told in Holy Scripture of three falls of Satan, the Evil Spirit. The first was in the beginning; the second, when the Gospel and the Kingdom of Heaven were preached to the world; the third will be at the end of all things. The first is told us by St. John the Evangelist. He says: "There was a great battle in heaven. Michael and his Angels fought with the dragon, and the dragon fought, and his angels. And they prevailed not, neither was their place found any more in heaven. And that great dragon was cast out, the old serpent, who is called the devil and Satan." The second fall, at the time of the Gospel, is spoken of by our Lord when He says, "I saw Satan, like lightning, falling from heaven." And the third by the same St. John: "There came down fire from God out of heaven . . . and the devil . . . was cast into the pool of fire and brimstone."

These three falls—the past, the present, and the future—the Evil Spirit had in mind when he moved Judas to betray our Lord. This was just his hour. Our Lord, when He was seized, said to His enemies, "This is your hour and the power of darkness." Satan knew his time was short and thought he might use it to good effect. But, little dreaming that he would be acting on behalf of the world's redemption, which our Lord's passion and death were to work out, in revenge, and, as he thought, in triumph, he smote Him once, he smote Him twice, he smote Him thrice, each successive time a heavier blow. The weight of the Cross, the barbarity of the soldiers and the crowd, were but his instruments. O Jesus, the only-begotten Son of God, the Word Incarnate, we praise, adore, and love You for Your ineffable condescension, even to allow Yourself thus for a time to fall into the hands and under the power of the Enemy of God and man, in order thereby to save us from being his servants and companions for eternity.

Our Father, Hail Mary, Glory Be.

V. Have Mercy upon us O Lord.
R. Have Mercy on us.

May the souls of the faithful departed, through the mercy of God, rest in peace.

The Tenth Station

JESUS IS STRIPPED OF HIS GARMENTS

V. Adoramus te, Christe, et benedicimus tibi.
R. Quia per sanctam Crucem tuam redemisti mundum.

V. We adore Thee O Christ and we praise Thee. (*Genuflect*)
R. Because by Thy Holy Cross Thou hast redeemed the world.

At last He has arrived at the place of sacrifice, and they begin to prepare Him for the Cross. His garments are torn from His bleeding body, and He, the Holy of

Holiest, stands exposed to the gaze of the coarse and scoffing multitude.

O You who in Your Passion was stripped of all Your clothes, and held up to the curiosity and mockery of the rabble, strip me of myself here and now, that on the Last Day I shall not come to shame before men and Angels. You endured the shame on Calvary that I might be spared the shame at the Judgment. You had nothing to be ashamed of personally, and the shame which You did feel was because You had taken man's nature upon Yourself. When they took Your garments from You, those innocent limbs were but objects of humble and loving adoration to the highest Seraphim. They stood around in speechless awe, wondering at Your beauty, and trembled at Your infinite self-abasement. But I, O Lord, how shall I appear if You will, hereafter, hold me up to be gazed upon, stripped of that robe of grace which is Yours, and my own personal life is seen for what it is? O how hideous I am in myself, even in my best estate. Even when I am cleansed from my mortal sins, what disease and corruption is seen even in my venial sins. How shall I be fit for the society of Angels, how for Your presence, until You burn this foul leprosy away in the fire of Purgatory?

Our Father, Hail Mary, Glory Be.

V. Have Mercy upon us O Lord.
R. Have Mercy on us.

May the souls of the faithful departed, through the mercy of God, rest in peace.

The Eleventh Station

JESUS IS NAILED TO THE CROSS

V. Adoramus te, Christe, et benedicimus tibi.
R. Quia per sanctam Crucem tuam redemisti mundum.

V. We adore Thee O Christ and we praise Thee. (*Genuflect*)
R. Because by Thy Holy Cross Thou hast redeemed the world.

The cross is laid on the ground, and Jesus stretched upon it, and then, swaying heavily to and fro, it is, after much exertion, jerked into the hole ready to receive it. Or, as others think, it is set upright, and Jesus is raised up and fastened to it. As the savage executioners drive in the huge nails, He offers Himself to the Eternal Father as a ransom for the world. The blows are struck—the blood gushes forth.

Yes, they set up the Cross on high, and they placed a ladder against it, and, having stripped Him of His garments, made Him mount. With His hands feebly grasping its sides and cross-woods, and His feet slowly, uncertainly, with much effort, with many slips, mounting up, the soldiers propped Him on each side, or He would have fallen. When He reached the projection where His sacred feet were to be, He turned around with sweet modesty and gentleness toward the fierce rabble, stretching out His arms as if He would embrace them. Then He lovingly placed the backs of His hands close against the transverse beam, waiting for the executioners to come with their sharp nails and heavy hammers to dig into the palms of His hands and to fasten them securely to the wood. There He hung, a perplexity to the multitude, a terror to evil spirits, the wonder, the awe, yet the joy, the adoration of the Holy Angels.

Our Father, Hail Mary, Glory Be.

V. Have Mercy upon us O Lord.
R. Have Mercy on us.

May the souls of the faithful departed, through the mercy of God, rest in peace.

The Twelfth Station

JESUS DIES UPON THE CROSS

V. Adoramus te, Christe, et benedicimus tibi.
R. Quia per sanctam Crucem tuam redemisti mundum.

V. We adore Thee O Christ and we praise Thee. (*Genuflect*)
R. Because by Thy Holy Cross Thou hast redeemed the world.

Jesus hung for three hours. During this time, He prayed for His murderers, promised Paradise to the penitent robber, and committed His Blessed Mother to the guardianship of St. John. Then all was finished, and He bowed His head and gave up His Spirit.

The worst is over. The Holiest is dead and departed. The most tender, the most affectionate, the holiest of the sons of men is gone. Jesus is dead, and with His death my sin shall die. I protest once for all, before men and Angels, that sin shall no more have dominion over me. This Lent I make myself God's own forever. The salvation of my soul shall be my first concern. With the aid of His grace I will create in me a deep hatred and sorrow for my past sins. I will try hard to detest sin, as much as I have ever loved it. Into God's hands I put myself, not by halves, but unreservedly. I promise You, O Lord, with the help of Your grace, to keep out of the way of temptation, to avoid all occasions of sin, to turn at once from the voice of the Evil One, to be regular in my prayers, so to die to sin that You will not have died for me on the Cross in vain.

Our Father, Hail Mary, Glory Be.

V. Have Mercy upon us O Lord.
R. Have Mercy on us.

May the souls of the faithful departed, through the mercy of God, rest in peace.

The Thirteenth Station

JESUS IS TAKEN FROM THE CROSS

V. Adoramus te, Christe, et benedicimus tibi.
R. Quia per sanctam Crucem tuam redemisti mundum.

V. We adore Thee O Christ and we praise Thee. (*Genuflect*)
R. Because by Thy Holy Cross Thou hast redeemed the world.

The multitude have gone home. Calvary is left solitary and still, except that St. John and the holy women are there. Then come Joseph of Arimathea and Nicodemus, who take down from the Cross the body of Jesus and place it in the arms of Mary.

O Mary, at last you are free to take your Son. Now, when His enemies can do no more, they leave Him in contempt to you. As His unexpected friends perform their difficult work, you look on with unspeakable thoughts. Your heart is pierced with the sword of which Simeon spoke. O Mother most sorrowful! Yet in your sorrow, there is a still greater joy. The joy in prospect nerved you to stand by Him as He hung upon the Cross; much more now, without swooning, without trembling, you receive Him to thy arms and on thy lap. Now you are supremely happy as having Him, though He comes to you not as He went from you. He went from your home, O Mother of God, in the strength and beauty of His manhood, and He comes back to you dislocated, torn to pieces, mangled, dead. Yet, O Blessed Mary, you are happier in this hour of woe than on the day of the marriage feast, for then He was leaving you, and now, in the future, as a Risen Savior, He will be separated from you no more.

Our Father, Hail Mary, Glory Be.

V. Have Mercy upon us O Lord.
R. Have Mercy on us.

May the souls of the faithful departed, through the mercy of God, rest in peace.

The Fourteenth Station

JESUS IS LAID IN THE TOMB

V. Adoramus te, Christe, et benedicimus tibi.
R. Quia per sanctam Crucem tuam redemisti mundum.

V. We adore Thee O Christ and we praise Thee. (*Genuflect*)
R. Because by Thy Holy Cross Thou hast redeemed the world.

But for a short three days, for a day and a half—Mary then must give Him up. He is not yet risen. His friends and servants take Him from you and place Him in an honorable tomb. They close it safely until the hour of His resurrection.

Lie down and sleep in peace in the calm grave for a little while, dear Lord, and then wake up for an everlasting reign. We, like the faithful women, will watch around You, for all our treasure, all our life, is lodged with You. And when our turn comes to die, grant, sweet Lord, that we may sleep calmly too, the sleep of the just. Let us sleep peacefully for the brief interval between death and the general resurrection. Guard us from the enemy; save us from the pit. Let our friends remember us and pray for us, O dear Lord. Let Masses be said for us, so that the pains of Purgatory, so much deserved by us and therefore so truly welcomed by us, may be over with little delay. Give us seasons of refreshment there; wrap us round with holy dreams and soothing contemplations while we gather strength to ascend the heavens. And then let our faithful guardian Angels help us up the glorious ladder, reaching from earth to heaven, which Jacob saw in vision. And when we reach the everlasting gates, let them open upon us with the music of Angels; and let St. Peter receive us, and our Lady, the glorious Queen of Saints, embrace us, and bring us to You, and to Your Eternal Father, and to Your Co-equal Spirit, Three Persons, One God, to reign with Them for ever and ever.

Our Father, Hail Mary, Glory Be.

V. Have Mercy upon us O Lord.
R. Have Mercy on us.

May the souls of the faithful departed, through the mercy of God, rest in peace.

WAY OF THE CROSS

According to the Visions of

BLESSED ANNE CATHERINE EMMERICH

The First Station

JESUS IS CONDEMNED TO DEATH

Excerpts from The Dolorous Passion of Our Lord Jesus Christ

Leader: "Pilate first spoke some words in which, with high-sounding titles, he named the Emperor Claudius Tiberius. Then he set forth the accusation against Jesus; that, as a seditious character, a disturber and violator of the Jewish laws, who had allowed Himself to be called the Son of God and the King of the Jews, He had been sentenced to death by the High Priests, and by the unanimous voice of the people given over to be crucified. Furthermore, Pilate, that iniquitous judge, who had in these last hours so frequently and publicly asserted the innocence of Jesus, now proclaimed that he found the sentence of the High Priests just, and ended with the words: 'I also condemn Jesus of Nazareth, King of the Jews to be nailed to the cross.' [. . .] The most afflicted Mother of Jesus, the Son of God, on hearing Pilate's words became like one in a dying state, for now was the cruel, frightful, ignominious death of her holy and beloved Son and Savior certain." (235–36)

Reflection

Leader: So many found Jesus guilty. They brought false accusations against Him. They misrepresented the truth. All of these people have judged the one who is the Judge of the world. Each of us will stand before the crucified One at our death and will be given an account of our lives. The Lord will ask us why we chose sinful actions. Jesus was condemned for no reason. We are condemned because of the evil we have done. Yet our Savior and Judge offers us redemption. We still have time to repent and amend our lives before we experience our own judgement.

Prayer

All: By the grace of Jesus's condemnation, grant me, O Lord, a heart contrite and humbled. Amen.

The Second Station

JESUS TAKES UP HIS CROSS

Excerpt

Leader: "As soon as the cross was thrown on the ground before Him, Jesus fell on His knees, put His arms around it, and kissed it three times while softly uttering a prayer of thanksgiving to His Heavenly Father for the redemption of mankind now begun. [. . .] But the executioners dragged Jesus up to a kneeling posture; and with difficult and little help He was forced to take the heavy beams upon His right shoulder and hold them fast with His right arm. I saw invisible angels helping Him, otherwise He would have been unable to lift the cross from the ground." (241)

Reflection

Leader: Jesus never gives up in praying to His Father. He knows for what purpose He is undergoing the passion. He prays for all people, past, present, and future, that they will appreciate and accept the grace of redemption. He was praying for conversion. The Passion of Jesus has already been brutal, with the scourging and crowning. Even with all He experienced, He was able to give thanks to God, the Father, for the work that He will accomplish. Angels always surrounded Jesus in His life, ministry, and passion. The angels surround us, too. Our Guardian Angel never departs from our side. The angels are present at every Mass. Let us become more aware of the invisible realities and graces in which we believe.

Prayer

All: By the grace of Jesus taking up His cross, O Lord, send Your angels to strengthen me when I face trials. Amen.

The Third Station

JESUS FALLS THE FIRST TIME

Excerpt

Leader: "Just here, where the street begins to ascend, there was a hollow place often filled, after a rain, with mud and water. In it, as in many such places in the streets of Jerusalem, lay a large stone to facilitate crossing. Poor Jesus, on reaching this spot with His heavy burden, could go no farther. The executioners pulled Him by the cords and pushed Him unmercifully.

Then did the Divine Cross-bearer fall full length on the ground by the projecting stone, His burden at His side. The drivers, with curses, pulled Him and kicked Him." (246)

Reflection

Leader: Jesus is exhausted, in unimaginable pain, shuffling His feet along to accomplish the Father's will. Jesus, carrying the heavy weight of the cross, becomes stuck in the mud and stumbles over the stone in the pathway. It is easy for anyone to fall or stumble, but much easier in Jesus's condition. In our lives, we will have our falls, not just literally, but the little stumbles along the path of Christian discipleship. Like Jesus, we will need to garner our strength, pick up the cross, and continue on our way.

Prayer

All: By the grace of Jesus's first fall, O Lord, help me to follow the gospel without stumbling. Amen.

The Fourth Station

JESUS MEETS HIS AFFLICTED MOTHER

Excerpt

Leader: "From His sunken eyes full of blood He cast, from under the tangled and twisted thorns of His crown, frightful to behold, a look full of earnest tenderness upon His afflicted Mother, and for the second time tottered under the weight of the cross and sank on His hands and knees to the ground. The most sorrowful Mother, in vehemence of her love and anguish, saw neither soldiers nor executioners—saw only her beloved, suffering, maltreated Son. Wringing her hands, she sprang over the couple of steps between the gateway and the executioners in advances, and rushing to Jesus, fell on her knees with her arms around Him. I heard, but I know not whether spoken with the lips or in spirit, the words: 'My Son!'—'My Mother!'" (248–49)

Reflection

Leader: In writing about the passion, Anne Catherine Emmerich repeatedly iterates that Mary interiorly participates in the passion. That Jesus and Mary are united, and she feels what He feels. She searched for Jesus while He was in the praetorium with Pilate, and now, she has a quick encounter with Him during the way of the cross. Just as they jeered and mocked Jesus, some did the same to Our Lady. Her consoling moment is to see her Son. By her presence, Jesus is able to look into the eyes that loved Him. This gives Him strength to press forward.

Prayer

All: O Lord, by the grace of Jesus meeting His Mother, may she meet me along the path of life, to encourage and intercede for me. Amen.

The Fifth Station

SIMON OF CYRENE HELPS JESUS CARRY HIS CROSS

Excerpt

Leader: "A crowd of well-dressed people came along on their way to the Temple. They cried out in compassion: 'Alas! The poor creature is dying!' Confusion arose among the rabble, for they could not succeed in making Jesus rise. The pharisees leading the procession cried out to the soldiers: 'We shall not get Him to Calvary alive. You must hunt up someone to help Him carry the cross.' Just then appeared, coming straight down the middle of the street, Simon of Cyrene, a pagan, followed by his three sons. He was carrying a bundle of sprigs under his arm, for he was a gardener . . . Simon was filled with disgust and repugnance for the task imposed upon him. Poor Jesus looked so horribly miserable, so awfully disfigured, and His garments were covered with mud; but He was weeping; and He cast upon a Simon a glance that roused his compassion. He had to help Him up. . . . He walked close behind Jesus, thus greatly lightening His burden." (250–51)

Reflection

Leader: At times, we might feel a little bit like Simon, annoyed that we are being asked to help someone. But then, as we do, our heart softens, and we become more receptive to the person, who may even be helping us individually in ways unknown to us. Jesus looks at Simon, and that compels him to help. Imagine yourself in the crowd, and Jesus looks at you. What does His glance do for you and your soul? What was Simon's life like following this chance encounter with the Savior?

Prayer

All: By the grace of Simon helping Jesus, O Lord, give me the courage to help someone without complaining and counting the cost. Amen.

The Sixth Station

Veronica Wipes the Face of Jesus

Excerpt

Leader: "It was Seraphia, the wife of Sirach, one of the members of the Council belonging to the Temple. Owing to her action of this day, she received the name of Veronica from *vera* (true) and *icon* (picture, or image). [. . .] As the procession drew near, she stepped out into the street veiled, a linen cloth hanging over her shoulder. [. . .] She pressed through the mob running at the side of the procession, in through the soldiers and executioners, stepped before Jesus, fell on her knees, and held up to Him the outspread end of the linen kerchief, with these words of entreaty: 'Permit me to wipe the face of my Lord!' Jesus seized the kerchief with His left hand and, with the flat, open palm, pressed it against His bloodstained face. Then passing it still with the left hand toward the right, which was grasping the arm of the cross, He pressed it between both palms and handed it back to Seraphia with thanks. She kissed it, hid it beneath her mantle, where she pressed it to her heart, and arose to her feet." (252–53)

Reflection

Leader: Seraphia, as Anne Catherine Emmerich calls her, or Veronica, as we more readily know her, was inspired out of her devotion to the Lord to bring that cloth. She had been a follower of Jesus with the other women. Jesus receives her kindness. Both treasure this holy moment, a moment that Veronica would be able to return to again and again with this holy keepsake.

Prayer

All: By the grace of Veronica's gesture, O Lord, inspire in me sentiments of devotion to You. Amen.

The Seventh Station

JESUS FALLS THE SECOND TIME

Excerpt

Leader: "Jesus again sank fainting. He did not fall to the ground, because Simon, resting the end of the cross upon the earth, drew nearer and supported His bowed form." (258)

Reflection

Leader: Our stations of the cross recount three falls of Jesus. Anne Catherine Emmerich gives an account of seven different falls. Each fall of Jesus is significant. This fall of Jesus comes after Simon begins to help Him. And from what Anne Catherine Emmerich saw, Simon stayed with Jesus for a while to help. His help in this moment prevented a greater fall of Jesus. When we fall, we need the support of family and friends to help us back up.

Prayer

All: By the grace of Jesus's second fall, O Lord, grant me a greater appreciation for the people who surround me and help me back up during life's troubles. Amen.

The Eighth Station

JESUS CONSOLES THE WEEPING WOMEN OF JERUSALEM

Excerpt

Leader: "At sight of His countenance so utterly wretched, the women raised a loud cry of sorrow and pity and, after the Jewish manner of showing compassion, extended toward Him kerchiefs with which to wipe off the perspiration. At this Jesus turned to them and said: 'Daughters of Jerusalem' (which meant, also, people from other Jewish cities), 'weep not over Me, but weep for yourselves and for your children.' [. . .] Jesus said some other beautiful words to the women [. . .] Among them, however, I remember these: 'Your tears shall be rewarded. Henceforth, ye shall tread another path.'" (258–59)

Reflection

Leader: When was the last time you cried? What have you shed tears over? Was it from joy and laughter? From hurt and pain? For whom have you shed tears? Your spouse, family, friends? The Lord sees your tears. And as He said to those women, He says to you, "Your tears shall be rewarded." Offer your tears to the Lord as a prayer.

Prayer

All: By the grace of Jesus consoling the women of Jerusalem, O Lord, may I be consoled by the words of Jesus and the hope of what is to come. Amen.

The Ninth Station

JESUS FALLS THE THIRD TIME

Excerpt

Leader: "The procession again moved onward. With blows and violent jerking at the cords that bound Him, Jesus was driven up the rough, uneven path between the city wall and Mount Calvary toward the north. At a spot where the winding path in its ascent turned toward the south, poor Jesus fell again for the sixth time. But His tormentors beat Him and drove Him on more rudely than ever until He reached the top of the rock, the place of execution, when with the cross He fell heavily to the earth for the seventh time." (259)

Reflection

Leader: He fell heavily to the earth. How many gashes and wounds Jesus must have endured during this gruesome passion? And when He was down on the ground, the soldiers could not contain themselves and beat Him further, as if all He had suffered was not enough. How easy it is for us to beat down somebody with words or judgments when life has gotten them down.

Prayer

All: By the grace of Jesus's third fall, O, Lord, may you change my heart, so that I will never cause anyone pain or hurt. Amen.

The Tenth Station

JESUS IS STRIPPED OF HIS GARMENTS

Excerpt

Leader: "And now the executioners tore from Our Lord the mantle they had flung around His shoulders. They next removed the fetter-girdle along with His own, and dragged the white woolen tunic over His head. Down the breast it had a slit bound with leather. When they wanted to remove the brown, seamless robe that His Blessed Mother had knit for Him, they could not draw it over His head, on account of the projecting crown of thorns. They consequently tore the crown again from His head, opening all the wounds afresh, tucked up the woven tunic and, with words of imprecation and insult, pulled it over His wounded and bleeding head. There stood the Son of Man, trembling in every limb, covered with blood and welts; covered with wounds, some closed, some bleeding; covered with scars and bruises! [. . .] The wool of the scapular was dried fast in His wounds and cemented with blood into the new and deep one made by the heavy cross upon His shoulder. This last wound caused Jesus unspeakable suffering." (266–67)

Reflection

Leader: The tunic, made by Our Lady, no longer retains its original color, for it is covered in His blood. How Jesus was able to endure all of this and still be standing, as the guards humiliated Him in His stripping and renewed His pain in each wound, is unimaginable and unexplainable. What suffering He endured for us!

Prayer

All: By the grace of Jesus being stripped of His garments, O Lord, grant me to share a little in His suffering, and move me to gratitude. Amen.

The Eleventh Station

JESUS IS NAILED TO THE CROSS

Excerpt

Leader: "The nails, at the sight of which Jesus shuddered, were so long that when the executioners grasped them in their fists, they projected about an inch at either end. [. . .] After nailing Our Lord's right hand, the crucifers found that His left, which also was fastened to the cross piece, did not reach to the hole made for the nail, for they had bored a good two inches from the fingertips. They consequently unbound Jesus's arm from the cross, wound cords around it, with their feet supported firmly against the cross, pulled it forward until the hand reached the hole. Now, kneeling on the arm and breast of the Lord, they fasted the arm again on the beam, and hammered the second nail through the left hand. The blood spurted up and Jesus's sweet, clear cry of agony sounded above the strokes of the heavy hammer. [. . .] The nailing of the feet was the most horrible of all, on account of the distension of the whole body. I counted thirty-six strokes of the hammer amid the poor Redeemer's moans. [. . .] Jesus's moans were purely cries of pain. Mingled with them were uninterrupted prayers, passages from the Psalms and Prophecies, whose predictions He was now fulfilling." (269–72)

Reflection

Leader: The torture of Jesus has not ended yet. If pounding the nails was not enough, they had to contort His body in order to accommodate the crucifixion. As I hear the pounding of the nails and hear the moaning of Jesus, I will never forget that He was thinking of me and all humankind. In this exhaustion, pain, and terrible condition, He still continues to commune with His Father in prayer. And Mary unites with Jesus, offering her prayers to the Father too. I know that Jesus had to go through this to fulfill what was spoken, but how I wish He did not have to die so cruelly.

Prayer

All: By the grace of Jesus being nailed to the cross, O Lord, grant me true repentance for the sins of my past and a firm purpose of amendment. Amen.

The Twelfth Station

JESUS DIES ON THE CROSS

Excerpt

Leader: "The hour of the Lord was now come. He was struggling with death, and a cold sweat burst out on every limb. John was standing by the cross and wiping Jesus's feet with his handkerchief. Magdalen, utterly crushed with grief, was leaning at the back of the cross. The Blessed Virgin, supported in the arms of Mary Cleophas and Salome, was standing between Jesus and the cross of the good thief, her gaze fixed upon her dying Son. Jesus spoke: 'It is consummated!' and raising His head He cried with a loud voice: 'Father, into Thy hands I commend My Spirit!' The sweet, loud cry rang through Heaven and earth. Then He bowed His head and gave up the Ghost. I saw His soul like a luminous phantom descending through the earth near the cross down to the sphere of Limbo.[1] John and the holy women sank, face downward, prostrate on the earth." (294)

Reflection

Leader: Three dedicated and devoted persons stand beneath the cross—His Mother, the beloved disciple, and Mary Magdalene. When He was a young boy, Jesus said that He had to be about His Father's business, and now, handing over His spirit, He would return to the Father's house. Jesus was sent to earth with a salvific mission. After a lengthy ordeal, the suffering servant accomplished the purpose for which He was sent. And His mission continued as He descended to lead forth so many souls to paradise, promised also to the Good Thief.

Prayer

All: By the grace of Jesus's death on the cross, O Lord, may I one day attain everlasting paradise and be among the angels and saints adoring You for all eternity. Amen.

---

1 By Limbo, Anne Catherine Emmerich means the place of the pre-redeemed, the netherworld, or Sheol.

The Thirteenth Station

JESUS IS TAKEN DOWN FROM THE CROSS

Excerpt

Leader: "It was still cloudy and foggy when they reached Mount Calvary, where they found their servants and the holy women, the latter sitting in front of the cross and in tears. Cassius and several converted soldiers stood like changed men, timidly and reverently, at some distance. Joseph and Nicodemus told the holy women and John of all that they had done to save Jesus from the ignominious death inflicted upon the thieves, and heard from them in return with what difficulty they had warded off the breaking of the Lord's bones, and how the Prophecy had been fulfilled. They told also of how Cassius had pierced the Sacred Body with his lance. As soon as the Centurion Abenadar arrived, they began sadly and reverently that most holy labor of love, the taking down from the cross and preparing for burial of the Sacred Body of their Master, their Lord, their Redeemer. (324)

"As soon as the Sacred Body was taken down, the men wrapped it in linen from the knees to the waist, and laid it on a sheet in His Mother's arms which, in anguish of heart and ardent longing, were stretched out to receive it." (326)

Reflection

Leader: The crucifixion was a horrible scene to look at, yet it was a beautiful scene at the same time. The two seem to be opposed, but the beauty lies in what was accomplished. How beautiful that some who were there came to confess faith in Jesus. Jesus must come down from the cross now, and reverently, these followers care for the body of the Savior. Devoutly and tenderly, they place the Son of God, and the Son of Joseph and Mary, into the arms of His mother, so that she can behold the One who came down from Heaven.

Prayer

All: By the grace of Jesus being taken down from the cross, O Lord, may we receive the strength to remain faithful in times of suffering and trust in the hope of the Resurrection. Amen.

The Fourteenth Station

JESUS IS PLACED IN THE HOLY SEPULCHER

Excerpt

Leader: "John once more conducted the Blessed Virgin and the other holy women to the sacred remains of Jesus. Mary knelt down by Jesus's head, took a fine linen scarf that hung around her neck under her mantle and which she had received from Claudia Procla, Pilate's wife, and laid it under the head of her Son. (334)

"The holy women sat down upon a seat opposite the

entrance of the grotto. The four men carried the Lord's body down into it, set it down, strewed the stone couch with sweet spices, spread over it a linen cloth, and deposited the sacred remains upon it. The cloth hung down over the couch. Then, having with tears and embraces given expression to their love for Jesus, they left the cave. The Blessed Virgin now went in, and I saw her sitting on the head of the tomb, which was about two feet from the ground. She was bending low over the corpse of her Child and weeping. When she left the cave, Magdalen hurried in with flowers and branches, which she had gathered in the garden and which she now scattered over the Sacred Body. She wrung her hands, and with tears and sighs embraced the feet of Jesus. When the men outside gave warning that it was time to close the doors, she went back to where the women were sitting." (338)

Reflection

Leader: Death does not stop one's love. The Blessed Virgin and Mary Magdalene still lovingly attend to the body of Jesus. The closing of the tomb means separation for a moment from the Lord. Our Lady maintains her hope from the words of Jesus. She knows that this is not her final good-bye, but that she and Jesus will be reunited soon in the resurrection.

Prayer

All: By the grace of Jesus being placed in the tomb, O Lord, may I never forget my loved ones who have passed away. Let their grave be a sign of hope for what awaits in eternity. Amen.

WAY OF THE CROSS

According to the Visions of

VENERABLE MARY OF JESUS OF ÁGREDA

The First Station

JESUS IS CONDEMNED TO DEATH BY PONTIUS PILATE

Excerpt from the Mystical City of God

Leader: "Pilate was much disturbed by the answers of Jesus and the obstinacy of the Jews. For on the one hand, seeing that they were so determined on the death of Jesus, he well knew, that it would be difficult to satisfy them without consenting to their demands; and on the other hand, he clearly saw that they persecuted Him out of mortal envy and that their accusations about His disturbing the people, were false and ridiculous. [. . .] By the light and grace which Pilate received, he became fully convinced that Jesus was truly innocent, although he never pierced the mystery of His Divinity and the greatness of His innocence." (597)

Reflection

Leader: Pilate was placed in a difficult situation and had reservations about the condemnation of Jesus. He was not strong enough to stand up to those who were bringing these false charges. Instead, he consented and caved to their wishes. While he believed Jesus was innocent, he still needed more in order to fully understand and believe in His Divinity.

Prayer

All: Dear Lord, give me the strength to stand up and speak when people are unjustly treated and condemned. Give me a deep faith, fully convicted, so I never waver from the truth that I have come to know from You. Amen.

The Second Station

JESUS CARRIES HIS CROSS

Excerpt

Leader: "Our Savior proceeded on the way to Calvary bearing upon His shoulders, according to the saying of Isaias, His own government and principality (Is. 9:6), which was none else than His Cross, from whence He was to subject and govern the world, meriting thereby that His name should be exalted above all other names and rescuing the human race from the tyrannical power of the demon over the sons of Adam (Col. 2:15). [. . .] In order to destroy this tyrant and break the scepter of his reign and the yoke of our servitude, Christ our Savior placed the Cross upon His shoulders; namely upon that place, where are borned both the yoke of slavery and the scepter of royal power." (654)

Reflection

Leader: They mockingly called Him a king, but He is our King, and this King reigns from the Cross, where He forgives and promises eternal life. The passion begins with that cross being picked up and carried on His shoulders. What is about to happen, Jesus willingly embraces.

Prayer

All: Jesus, the weight of the cross was heavy on Your shoulders. The weight I carry will never compare to what you endured. Help me carry my little crosses with humility and grace. Amen.

The Third Station

JESUS FALLS THE FIRST TIME

Excerpt

Leader: "The executioners, bare of all human compassion and kindness, dragged our Savior Jesus along with incredible cruelty and insults. Some of them jerked Him forward by the ropes in order to accelerate His passage, while others pulled from behind in order to retard it. On account of this jerking and the weight of the Cross, they caused Him to sway to and from and often to fall to the ground." (656)

Reflection

Leader: Jesus falls to the ground because of the way His executioners treat and torment Him. The cross becomes heavy, yes, because the wood is heavy, but because my sins make it heavy too. What does Jesus think of when He falls underneath the cross? He thinks of me. His passion was for me.

Prayer

All: Jesus, my words and prayers cannot begin to express how sorry I am for what You endured. Please let me never forget how You were treated and help me to never treat You or another person like that ever again. Amen.

The Fourth Station

JESUS MEETS HIS MOTHER

Excerpt

Leader: "From the house of Pilate the sorrowful and stricken Mother followed with the multitudes on the way of her Divine Son, accompanied by Saint John and the pious women. As the surging crowds hindered Her from getting very near to the Lord, she asked the eternal Father to be permitted to stand at the foot of the Cross of her blessed Son and see Him die with her own eyes. [. . .] The holy angels obeyed Her with great reverence; and they speedily led the Queen through some bystreet, in order that She might meet her Son. Thus, it came that both of them met face to face in sweetest recognition of each other and in mutual renewal of each other's interior sorrows. Yet they did not speak to one another, nor would the fierce cruelty of the executioners have permitted such an intercourse." (657)

Reflection

Leader: Mother and Son meet. They exchanged glances. Their souls are united in the passion. Mary feels the inner pain of Jesus. Jesus intensely loves His mother in this moment, and she realizes it and mutually loves Him to the same degree. I cannot imagine what she is thinking. But she is praying. And the Father hears her prayer.

Prayer

All: Heavenly Father, thank you for letting Mary and Jesus meet along the way. Please allow her to look down lovingly at me, just as she looked at her Son. As in your prayer to the Father then, please Mother Mary, pray for me now. Amen.

The Fifth Station

SIMON OF CYRENE HELPS JESUS CARRY THE CROSS

Excerpt

Leader: "In fulfillment of the prayerful wish of the Blessed Mother, the pharisees and ministers were inspired with the resolve to engage some man to help Jesus Our Savior in carrying the cross to Mount Calvary. At this juncture, Simon of Cyrene, the father of the disciples Alexander and Rufus (Mark 15:21), happened to come along. [. . .] This Simon was now forced by the Jews to carry the cross a part of the way. [. . .] The Cyrenean took hold of the cross and Jesus was made to follow between the two thieves, in order that all might believe Him to be a criminal and malefactor like to them." (660)

Reflection

Leader: Maria of Ágreda reveals a few interesting parts about the Way of the Cross here. She tells us that the two thieves, crucified alongside Jesus, were a part of this procession to Calvary. Second, she says that they forced Simon of Cyrene to carry the cross. If he was forced, how willing was he to help? Does helping Jesus for these moments transform his heart?

Prayer

All: Lord, if I was there, I hope that I would have willingly helped You. My love for You would force me to help You, not someone else threatening me. I can still help You today when I willingly choose to help the poor and marginalized. Wherever there is resistance in my heart, transform it to a willingness to serve. Amen.

The Sixth Station

VERONICA WIPES THE FACE OF JESUS

Excerpt[2]

Leader: "But when the procession had advanced about two hundred steps from the spot where Simon began to assist Our Lord in carrying His cross, the door of a

2 This station is borrowed from the Visions of Anne Catherine Emmerich (*The Dolorous Passion of Our Lord Jesus Christ* pp. 252–53), as Mary of Ágreda does not recount the meeting of Veronica and Our Lord in her mystical works.

beautiful house on the left opened, and a woman of majestic appearance, holding a young girl by the hand, came out, and walked up to the very head of the procession. Seraphia was the name of the brave woman who thus dared to confront the enraged multitude; she was the wife of Sirach, one of the councillors belonging to the Temple, and was afterwards known by the name Veronica, which name was given from the words vera icon (true portrait), to commemorate her brave conduct on this day.

"Those who were marching at the head of the procession tried to push Veronica back; but she made her way through the mob, the soldiers, and the archers, reached Jesus, fell on her knees before Him, and presented the veil, saying at the same time: 'Permit me to wipe the face of my Lord.' Jesus took the veil in His left hand, wiped His bleeding face, and returned it with thanks. Seraphia kisses it, and put it under her cloak."

Reflection

Leader: Veronica was inspired out of her devotion to the Lord to bring that cloth. She had been a follower of Jesus with the other women. Jesus receives her kindness. Both treasure this holy moment, a moment that Veronica would be able to return to again and again with this holy keepsake.

Prayer

All: Lord, grant me the courage to embrace You amid my own persecutions. Inspire in me a fervent love and deeper devotion to You. Amen.

The Seventh Station

JESUS FALLS THE SECOND TIME

Excerpt

Leader: "In His falls they pounced upon Him, inflicting blows and kicks, trampling upon His body and upon His head and face. All these deviltries they accompanied with festive shouts and opprobrious insults." (547)

Reflection

Leader: Who could kick the Lord and Savior of the world? A weak person, an ignorant person. Yet, every time His name is taken in vain, it is as if we inflict blows and kicks. The sacrilegious actions of unbelievers and those who blaspheme Jesus by words and actions are like beating the Lord when He has fallen. In His falls, He sees them, and knows for whom He suffers the passion.

Prayer

All: O Lord, by Your passion and fall, convert those who live their lives indifferent to You and Your teachings. I offer my sacrifices and prayers in atonement for the insults and blasphemies You continue to receive this day. Amen.

The Eighth Station

JESUS MEETS THE WOMEN OF JERUSALEM

Excerpt

Leader: "As the Evangelist tells us, there were other women among the crowds, who followed the Savior in bitter tears and lamentations (Luke 23:27). The sweetest Jesus turning toward them, addressed them and said: 'Daughters of Jerusalem, weep not over Me; but weep for yourselves and for your children.' [. . .] By these mysterious words the Lord acknowledged the tears shed on account of His Passion, and to a certain extent, by showing His appreciation of them, He approved of them. In these women He wished to teach us for what purpose our tears should be shed so that they may attain their end." (657)

Reflection

Leader: The passion and death of Jesus certainly is a cause for weeping and tears. But Jesus tells the women not to weep over Him but to weep for themselves and their children. Have you wept over your sinfulness? Your lack of faith? Tears are a sign of repentance. The Lord sees your tears and sorrow so that they may bring forgiveness.

Prayer

All: O Lord, grant me the grace of sincere contrition and true sorrow for the sins of my past life. My sins move me to tears. Let it lead to a greater trust in Your mercy and redemption. Amen.

The Ninth Station

JESUS FALLS THE THIRD TIME

Excerpt

Leader: "'All this I place in Thy hands as the true and almighty Lord and God. As far as My wishes are concerned, I suffer and die for all, and I desire that all shall be saved, under the condition that all follow Me and profit of my Redemption. Thus may they pass from the slavery of the devil to be Thy children, My brethren and co-heirs of the grace merited by Me. [. . .] And I pray for those who are persecuting Me, in order that they may be converted to the truth. Above all do I ask Thee for the exaltation of Thy ineffable and most holy name.'" (669)

Reflection

Leader: The passion and way of the cross is a means to get Jesus to Calvary, to be nailed to the cross, and die for us. The passion was also a time of intense prayer for Jesus. He prayed to His Father all throughout His passion, offering everything for the grace of redemption soon to be accomplished. In our falls throughout life, let us never stop praying. The Lord prayed for us that we would never give up. When you fall, pick up, seek mercy, and begin again.

Prayer

All: Jesus, I unite my prayers to Yours. By praying in union with You, I know that Your will shall be done. Set all those enslaved by the torments of the devil free from their bondage to sin. Convert those who do not believe. Let the name of Almighty God be forever praised. Amen.

The Tenth Station

JESUS IS STRIPPED OF HIS GARMENTS

Excerpt

Leader: "It was already the sixth hour, which corresponds to our noontime, and the executioners, intending to crucify the Savior naked, despoiled Him of the seamless tunic and of His garments. As the tunic was large and without opening in front, they pulled it over the head of Jesus without taking off the crown of thorns, but on the account of the rudeness with which they proceeded, they inhumanly tore off the crown with the tunic. Thus, they opened anew all the wounds of His head, and in some of them remained the thorns, which, in spite of their being so hard and sharp, were wrenched off by the violence with which the executioners despoiled Him of His tunic and, with it, of the crown. With heartless cruelty they again forced it down upon His sacred head, opening up wounds upon wounds." (667)

Reflection

Leader: Mystics, like Maria of Ágreda, help us realize the pain, suffering, and torment that Jesus went through. This description of Jesus's stripping is heart wrenching. He suffered so much. He suffered again and again. The wounds on His head and on His body will soon be glorified through the resurrection. What pain we must endure too until our glorification by the Lord.

Prayer

All: Jesus, my heart is full of sorrow thinking of all that You endured. My mind cannot even grasp how You were able to keep moving with all Your wounds and pains. I repent of all the times my sins have inflicted pain upon You. Give me a deep horror of sin so that I will stop offending You by my words and actions. Amen.

The Eleventh Station

JESUS IS NAILED TO THE CROSS

Excerpt

Leader: "Having bored the three holes into the Cross, the executioners again commanded Christ the Lord to stretch Himself out upon it in order to be nailed to it. The Supreme and Almighty King, as the Author of patience, obeyed, and at the will of the hangmen, placed Himself with outstretched arms upon the blessed wood. (672)

"Presently one of the executioners seized the hand of Jesus our Savior and placed it upon the auger-hole, while another hammered a large and rough nail through the palm. The veins and sinews were torn, and the bones of the sacred hand, which made the Heavens and all that exists, were forced apart." (673)

Reflection

Leader: Jesus knew the Father's plan. The God who created all on earth, including the tree from which this cross was formed, readily undergoes the next steps. He reaches out His arm and hand so that it can be nailed to the cross. He knows that in just a short time, His life and mission will be completed. His death on the cross will lead to new and everlasting life.

Prayer

All: Lord, help me to be more like You, willing to follow wherever You lead me, and to do whatever You want me to do. You went to Calvary to be crucified. Come to my aid, when I resist Your most holy will. Amen.

The Twelfth Station

JESUS DIES ON THE CROSS

Excerpt

Leader: "As the wood of the Cross was the throne of His majesty and the chair of the doctrine of life, and as He was now raised upon it, confirming His doctrine by His example, Christ now uttered those words of highest charity and perfection: 'Father, forgive them for they know not what they do!' (681)

"'Father, into Thy hands I commend my spirit.' The

Lord spoke these words in a loud and strong voice, so that the bystanders heard them. In pronouncing them He raised His eyes to Heaven, as one speaking with the Eternal Father, and with the last accent He gave up His spirit and inclined His head. By the divine force of these words Lucifer with all his demons were hurled into the deepest caverns of hell, there they lay motionless." (687)

Reflection

Leader: Jesus spoke seven phrases from the cross. Mary, the other women, and John stood below Jesus as He proclaimed His final words. They are words we must listen to and live by. He forgave, so I must forgive others. Forgiveness is hard. But Jesus endured all that He did and still wanted others to know they were forgiven. He uttered His last phrase, surrendering Himself to the Father who sent Him to earth.

Prayer

All: Jesus, I stand with Mary and John. I hear Your words. I see You take Your last breath. I am grateful that Your suffering is over. I wish to stay with Mary, and like John, to behold her as my mother. Thank You for what You have accomplished for me, a lowly sinner. Amen.

The Thirteenth Station

JESUS IS TAKEN DOWN FROM THE CROSS

Excerpt

Leader: "This wounding of the lance, which could not be felt by the sacred and dead body of the Lord, was felt by the most Blessed Mother in His stead and in the same manner as if her chaste bosom had been pierced. She said to Longinus: 'The almighty look upon thee with eyes of mercy for the pain thou hast caused to my soul!' [. . .] Thus it also happened; for the Savior, moved by the prayer of His blessed Mother, ordained that some of the blood and water from His sacred side should drop upon the face of Longinus and restore to him his eyesight, which he had almost lost. At the same time sight was given to his soul, so that he recognized in the Crucified his Savior, whom he had so inhumanly mutilated." (728)

Reflection

Leader: Before Jesus is taken down from the cross and placed in the arms of His mother, Longinus pierces His side. Mary felt the piercing. It's as if the prophecy of Simeon is being fulfilled on Calvary's hill, a sword has pierced her heart. Like Jesus, Mary persevered in prayer, offering in union with Jesus her prayer for the conversion of those who persecuted and crucified Jesus. Mary has always been an intercessor. She was then and is for us today. Longinus receives the gift of spiritual sight through Mary's prayers. May she still pray for us, so that we might be healed of whatever spiritual blindness afflicts our souls.

Prayer

All: Mary, you stood by Jesus as He hung on the cross. You prayed for so many people, people whose names you did not know at that time. Please pray for me today. You are the Mother of mercy and obtain many graces from Jesus. May the grace of the passion of Jesus be always at work in my life. Let me never forget all that He endured. Amen.

The Fourteenth Station

JESUS IS LAID IN THE TOMB

Excerpt

Leader: "Some time passed during which the sorrowful Mother held at her breast the dead Jesus, and as evening was far advancing, Saint John and Joseph besought her to allow the burial of her Son and God to proceed. The most prudent Mother yielded; and they now embalmed the sacred body. [. . .] All of them, in silence and in tears, joined the procession. They proceeded toward a nearby garden, where Joseph had hewn into the rock a new grave, in which nobody had as yet been buried or deposited (John 19:41). In this most blessed sepulchre they placed the sacred body of Jesus. Before they closed it up with the heavy stone, the devout and prudent Mother adored Christ anew, causing the admiration of men and angels. They imitated her, all of them adoring the crucified Savior now resting in His grave; thereupon they closed the sepulchre with the stone, which, according to the Evangelist, was very heavy (Matt 27:60)." (737)

Reflection

Leader: All throughout her life, Mary adored her Son. She adored Him in the manger. She adored Him in the home at Nazareth. She adored Him as He hung upon the cross. Now, she has this moment of adoration at the tomb. She is joined by those who surround her, and with the angels who ministered to her and Jesus. Words cannot capture what Mary would have thought at the moment of prayer. Surely, there was silence, pondering God's will. Certainly, prayers of affection and longing. Even in this sorrowful moment, Mary was filled with hope, because she knew what Jesus said would happen next, and so she held to her faith in what was to come.

Prayer

All: Jesus, I adore You in the tomb with Mary, who persevered in prayer. May I learn from her what it means to adore at a difficult time, to have faith when it would be easy to doubt, to have hope when I should despair, to love when it isn't easy. Because she walked the way of the cross, and now that I have walked with her, I want to be just a little bit more like her. Let it be so. Amen.

Let Us Pray:

O God, Who by the Precious Blood of Thy only-begotten Son didst sanctify the Standard of the Cross, grant, we beseech Thee, that we who rejoice in the glory of the same Holy Cross may at all times and places rejoice in Thy protection, Through the same Christ, our Lord.

End with one Our Father, Hail Mary, and Glory be, for the intentions of the Holy Father.

PSALM 129

1 Out of the depths I have cried to thee, O Lord:
2 Lord, hear my voice. Let thy ears be attentive to the voice of my supplication.
3 If thou, O Lord, wilt mark iniquities: Lord, who shall stand it.
4 For with thee there is merciful forgiveness: and by reason of thy law, I have waited for thee, O Lord.
My soul hath relied on his word:
5 my soul hath hoped in the Lord.
6 From the morning watch even until night, let Israel hope in the Lord.
7 Because with the Lord there is mercy: and with him plentiful redemption.
8 And he shall redeem Israel from all his iniquities.

V. Eternal rest grant unto them O Lord.
R. And let perpetual light shine on them.

May the Souls of the Faithful departed, through the Mercy of God, rest in peace. Amen.

STABAT MATER
(Concluding Hymn)

Virgo virginum praeclara,
Mihi jam non sis amara,
Fac me tecum plangere;

Virgin of all virgins best!
Listen to my fond request:
Let me share thy grief divine;

Fac, ut portem Christi mortem,
Passionis fac consortem,
Et plagas recolere.

Let me, to my latest breath,
In my body bear the death
Of that dying Son of thine.

Fac me plagis vulnerari,
Fac me cruce inebriari,
Et cruore Filii.

Wounded with His every wound,
Steep my soul till it hath swooned
In His very Blood away.

Flammis ne urar succensus
Per te, Virgo, sim defensus
In die judicii.

Be to me, O Virgin, nigh,
Lest in flames I burn and die,
In His awful Judgment Day.

Christe, cum sit hinc exire,
Da per Matrem me venire
Ad palman victoriae

Christ, when Thou shalt
call me hence,
Be Thy Mother my defense,
Be Thy cross my victory.

Quando corpus morietur,
Fac ut animae donetur
Paradisi gloria.
Amen.

While my body here decays,
May my soul Thy goodness praise,
Safe in paradise with Thee.
Amen.

V. Ora pro nobis, Virgo dolorosissima.
R. *Ut digni efficiamur promissionibus Christi.*

V. Pray for us, Virgin most sorrowful.
R. *That we may be made worthy of the promises of Christ.*

OREMUS

Interveniat pro nobis, quaesumus, Domine Jesu Christe, nunc et in hora mortis nostrae, apud tuam clementiam, beata Virgo Maria Mater tua, cujus sacratissimam animam in hora tuae passionis doloris gladius pertransivit. Per te, Jesu Christe, salvator mundi, qui cum Patre et Spiritu Sancto vivis et regnas, per omnia saecula saeculorum. *Amen.*

LET US PRAY

Grant, we beseech Thee, O Lord Jesus Christ, that the most blessed Virgin Mary, Thy Mother, through whose most holy soul, in the hour of Thine own Passion, the sword of sorrow passed, may intercede for us before the throne of Thy mercy, now and at the hour of our death. Through Thee, Jesus Christ, Saviour of the world, Who livest and reignest with the Father and the Holy Ghost, now and forever. *Amen.*

PRAYERS FOR MEDITATION FOLLOWING THE WAY OF THE CROSS

ACT OF RESIGNATION

MY LORD GOD, EVEN NOW I accept at Thy hands, cheerfully and willingly, with all its anxieties, pains and sufferings, whatever kind of death it shall please Thee to be mine. Amen.

ADORAMUS TE CHRISTI

Adoramus te, Christe,	*We adore Thee, O Christ,*
et benedicimus tibi,	*and we bless Thee,*
quia per sanctam crucem tuam	*who by Thy Holy Cross*
redemisti mundum.	*hast redeemed the world.*
Qui passus es pro nobis,	*Thou, who hast suffered death for us,*
Domine, Domine, miserere nobis.	*O Lord, O Lord, have mercy on us.*

PRAYER BEFORE THE CRUCIFIX

Look down upon me, good and gentle Jesus
while before Your face I humbly kneel and,
with burning soul,
pray and beseech You
to fix deep in my heart lively sentiments
of faith, hope, and charity;
true contrition for my sins,
and a firm purpose of amendment.
While I contemplate,
with great love and tender pity,
Your five most precious wounds,
pondering over them within me
and calling to mind the words which David,
Your prophet, said to You, my Jesus:
"They have pierced My hands and My feet,
they have numbered all My bones."
Amen.

ANIMA CHRISTI

Soul of Christ, sanctify me.
Body of Christ, save me.
Blood of Christ, embolden me.
Water from the side of Christ, wash me.
Passion of Christ, strengthen me.
O good Jesus, hear me.
Within your wounds hide me.
Never permit me to be parted from you.

From the evil Enemy defend me.
At the hour of my death call me
and bid me come to you,
that with your Saints I may praise you
for age upon age.
Amen.

THE JESUS PRAYER

Lord Jesus Christ, Son of God, have mercy on me a sinner. Amen.	Domine Iesu Christe, Fili Dei, miserere mei, peccatoris. Amen.

PRAYER TO JESUS CRUCIFIED

O my crucified Savior! Deign to listen favorably to the prayer I now address to Thee for the hour of my death, when the approach of that dreaded moment will render rue incapable of all sentiment.

O, Jesus, when my dying eyes can no longer look upon Thee, remember the loving glance I now cast upon Thee, and have mercy upon me!

When my parched lips can no longer kiss Thy sacred wounds, remember the kisses I now press upon them, and have mercy on me.

When my stiffening fingers can no longer hold the crucifix, remember the fervor with which I clasp it at this moment, and have mercy upon me.

When my swollen and motionless tongue can no longer pronounce a single word, remember the invocation

I now make to Thee, and have mercy upon me. Amen.

"Jesus, Mary, and Joseph, I recommend my soul to you."

PRAYER TO THE WOUNDED SIDE OF JESUS
(St. Gertrude)

O Lord Jesus, compassionate Pelican, who hast cleansed us in Thine own Blood, I give Thee thanks for the sweet and adorable Wound of love which Thou didst receive on the Cross when Thine all-conquering love opened Thy sweet-flowing side, and wounded Thy most Sacred Heart with an arrow of love. Blessed for ever be that life-giving stroke, and that hallowed wound, and blessed be the Adorable Blood and water of salvation which gushed forth from it, to wash away all our sins! I am all defiled, wash me, O compassionate Jesus! Pour upon me that all-efficacious water. I am weak, strengthen me by the unction of the Sacred Blood, and grant that, at my last hour, my portion and heritage may be but one drop of that Divine Stream. O most loving Jesus! By Thy pierced Heart, I pray Thee, wound my heart with that arrow of love, so that nothing earthly may ever again abide in it, but that it may be filled with Thy glowing love alone forever. Amen.

HOW TO GAIN A PARTIAL OR PLENARY INDULGENCE

To GAIN A PARTIAL INDULGENCE, a Catholic in good standing must simply perform the prescribed work—in this case, make the Way of the Cross—in the state of grace (that is, free of having committed a mortal sin that remains unforgiven in Confession) and have at least a general intention of gaining indulgences. A partial indulgence can be acquired more than once a day, unless otherwise expressly indicated. To gain a plenary indulgence, however, several additional factors must also be present. All together, they are the following:

1. *The person must be a Catholic, not excommunicated, and in the state of grace,* that is, free from mortal sin that has not been confessed and forgiven in the Sacrament of Penance.

2. *The recipient must go to Confession, receive Holy Communion, and say at least one Our Father and one Hail Mary for the intentions of the Sovereign Pontiff.* These can all be done several days before or after performing the prescribed "work," in this case, making the Way of the

Cross. But it is more fitting that the Communion and the prayers for the Pope's intentions be on the same day that the "work" is performed. A single Confession suffices for gaining several plenary indulgences, but sacramental Communion must be received and prayer for the intention of the Sovereign Pontiff must be recited for the gaining of each plenary indulgence.

3. *The recipient must be free from all attachment to sin, even venial sin.* Although a person might still sin, as we all do, or even be inclined to an habitual sin, such as using God's name in vain, yet so long as the attachment to the sin or the *desire* to commit it is absent from the person's soul, he or she would be considered "free from attachment to sin." (If this disposition is in any way less than perfect, or if any of the prescribed three conditions are not fulfilled, the indulgence will be only partial.)

4. *Only one plenary indulgence may be gained per day.* But one can obtain the plenary indulgence "for the moment of death," even if another plenary indulgence had been acquired on the same day.

5. *The person must perform the prescribed work,* in this case, make the Way of the Cross—*with at least the general intention of gaining indulgences.* In making the Way of the Cross, the following norms apply:

a. The pious exercise must be made before stations of the Way of the Cross legitimately erected.

b. For the erection of the Way of the Cross, fourteen crosses are required, to which it is customary to add fourteen pictures or images, which represent the stations of Jerusalem.

c. Although, according to the more common practice, the pious exercise consists of fourteen pious readings to which some vocal prayers are added, nothing more is required than a pious meditation on the Passion and Death of the Lord, which need not be a particular consideration of the individual mysteries of the stations.

d. A movement from one station to the next is required, but if the pious exercise is made publicly and if it is not possible for all taking part to go in an orderly way from station to station, it suffices if at least the one conducting the exercise goes from station to station, the others remaining in their places.

e. Those who are "impeded" can gain the same indulgence if they spend at least a half hour in pious reading and meditation on the Passion and Death of Our Lord Jesus Christ.[3]

---

3 The above was taken from the Enchiridion of Indulgences—Norms and Grants, authorized English Edition, translated by Fr. William T. Barry, C.SS.R., Catholic Book Publishing Co., New York, from the Second Revised Edition of the Enchiridion Indulgentiarum issued by the Sacred Apostolic Penitentiary, 1968 and originally published by Libreria Editrice Vaticana, Vatican City, 1968.

Appendix

TRADITIONAL HYMNS SUNG DURING LENT AND PASSIONTIDE

Ave Verum

Wolfgang Amadeus Mozart

Ave verum Corpus natum de Maria Virgine:
Vere passum immolatum in cruce pro homine:
Cuius latus perforatum fluxit aqua et sanguine:
Esto nobis praegustatum mortis in examine.
O Jesu dulcis!
O Jesu pie!
O Jesu fili Mariae.

Hail, true Body, born of the Virgin Mary,
the very Body which suffered and was sacrificed
on the cross for humankind,
and whose pierced side overflowed with water and blood:
In the agony of death be for us a foretaste of heaven,
O kind and loving Jesus, son of Mary.

Adore Te Devote

St. Thomas Aquinas

Adoro te devote, latens Deitas,
Quae sub his figuris vere latitas:
Tibi se cor meum totum subicit,
Quia te contemplans totum deficit.

Visus, tactus, gustus in te fallitur,
Sed auditus solo tuto creditur:
Credo quidquid dixit Dei Filius:
Nil hoc verbo veritatis verbo verius.

In cruce latebat sola Deitas,
At hic latet simul et humanitas:
Ambo tamen credens atque confitens,
Peto quod petivit latro paenitens.

Plagas, sicut Thomas, non intueor:
Deum tamen meum te confiteor:
Fac me tibi semper magis credere,
In te spem habere, te diligere.

O memoriale mortis Domini,
Panis vivus vitam praestans homini,
Praesta mean menti de te vivere,
Et te illi semper dulce sapere.

Pie pellicane, Jesu Domine,
Me immundum munda tuo sanguine,
Cuius una stilla salvum facere

Totum mundum quit ab omni scelere.

Jesu, quem velatum nunc aspicio,
Oro fiat illud quod tam sitio:
Ut te revelata cernens facie,
Visu sim beátus tuae gloriae.

O Godhead hid, devoutly I adore Thee,
Who truly art within the forms before me;
To Thee my heart I bow with bended knee,
As failing quite in contemplating Thee.

Sight, touch, and taste in Thee are each deceived;
The ear alone most safely is believed:
I believe all the Son of God has spoken,
Than Truth's own word there is no truer token.

God only on the Cross lay hid from view;
But here lies hid at once the Manhood too:
And I, in both professing my belief,
Make the same prayer as the repentant thief.

Thy wounds, as Thomas saw, I do not see;
Yet Thee confess my Lord and God to be:
Make me believe Thee ever more and more;
In Thee my hope, in Thee my love to store.

O thou Memorial of our Lord's own dying!
O Bread that living art and vivifying!
Make ever Thou my soul on Thee to live;
Ever a taste of Heavenly sweetness give.

O loving Pelican! O Jesu, Lord!
Unclean I am, but cleanse me in Thy Blood;
Of which a single drop, for sinners spilt,
Is ransom for a world's entire guilt.

Jesu! Whom for the present veil'd I see,
What I so thirst for, O vouchsafe to me:
That I may see Thy countenance unfolding,
And may be blest Thy glory in beholding. Amen.

Pange Lingua

St. Thomas Aquinas

Pange, lingua, gloriosi
Corporis mysterium
Sanguinisque pretiosi,
Quem in mundi pretium
Fructus ventris generosi
Rex effudit gentium.

Nobis datus, nobis natus
Ex intacta Virgine,
Et in mundo conversatus,
Sparso verbi semine,
Sui moras incolatus
Miro clausit ordine.

In supremae nocte coenae,
Recumbens cum fratribus,
Observata lege plene

Cibis in legalibus,
Cibum turbae duodenae
Se dat suis manibus.

Verbum caro, panem verum
Verbo carnem efficit:
Fitque sanguis Christi merum,
Et si sensus deficit,
Ad firmandum cor sincerum
Sola fides sufficit.

Tantum ergo Sacramentum
Veneremur cernui:
Et antiquum documentum
Novo cedat ritui;
Praestet fides supplementum
Sensuum defectui.

Genitori, Genitoque
Laus et jubilatio,
Salus, honor, virtus quoque
Sit et benedictio:
Procedenti ab utroque
Compar sit laudatio.
Amen.

Sing, my tongue, the Savior's glory,
Of his flesh the myst'ry sing;
Of the blood, all price exceeding,
Shed by our immortal King,

Destined for the world's redemption,
From a noble womb to spring.

Of a pure and spotless virgin
Born for us on Earth below,
He, as God with humans mingling,
Stayed, the seeds of truth to sow,
Then he closed in solemn order
Wondrously his life of woe.

On the night of that Last Supper,
Seated with his chosen band,
He, the Paschal victim eating,
First fulfills the Law's command,
Then as food to his apostles
Gives himself with his own hand.

Now in adoration coming
To the sacred Host we hail;
Lo! o'er ancient forms departing,
Newer rites of grace prevail;
Faith, for all defects supplying,
Where the feeble senses fail.

When I Survey the Wondrous Cross

Isaac Watts (1707)

When I survey the wondrous cross On which the Prince of glory died, My richest gain I count but loss, And pour contempt on all my pride.

Forbid it, Lord, that I should boast, Save in the death of Christ my God! All the vain things that charm me most, I sacrifice them to His blood.

See from His head, His hands, His feet, Sorrow and love flow mingled down! Did e'er such love and sorrow meet, Or thorns compose so rich a crown?

His dying crimson, like a robe, Spreads o'er His body on the tree; Then I am dead to all the globe, And all the globe is dead to me.

Were the whole realm of nature mine, That were a present far too small; Love so amazing, so divine, Demands my soul, my life, my all.

O Sacred Head, Surrounded

Attributed to St. Bernard of Clairvaux

O sacred Head surrounded
By crown of piercing thorn!
O bleeding Head, so wounded,
Reviled and put to scorn!
The pow'r of death comes o'er you,
The glow of life decays,
Yet angel hosts adore you
And tremble as they gaze.

I see your strength and vigor
All fading in the strife,
And death with cruel rigor,

Bereaving you of life;
O agony and dying!
O love to sinners free!
Jesus, all grace supplying,
O turn your face on me.

In this, your bitter passion,
Good Shepherd, think of me
With your most sweet compassion,
Unworthy though I be:
Beneath your cross abiding
For ever would I rest,
In your dear love confiding,
And with your presence blest.

Lord, Who Throughout These Forty Days

Lord, who throughout these forty days,
For us did fast and pray,
Teach us with you to mourn our sins,
And close by you to stay.

As you with Satan did contend,
And did the vict'ry win,
O give us strength in you to fight,
In you to conquer sin.

As you did hunger bear and thirst,
So teach us, gracious Lord,
To die to self, and always live
By your most holy word.

And through these days of penitence,
And through your Passion-tide,
Forevermore, in life and death,
O Lord, with us abide.

Abide with us that when this life
Of suffering is past,
An Easter of unending joy
We may attain at last!

The Glory of These Forty Days

Pope Gregory I. Translated by Maurice F. Bell (1906)

The glory of these forty days
we celebrate with songs of praise,
for Christ, by whom all things were made,
himself has fasted and has prayed.

Alone and fasting Moses saw
the loving God who gave the law.
And to Elijah, fasting, came
the steed and chariots of flame.

So Daniel trained his mystic sight,
delivered from the lion's might.
And John, the Savior's friend, became
the herald of Messiah's name.

Then grant, O God, that we may, too,
return in fast and prayer to you.
Our spirits strengthen with your grace,
and give us joy to see your face.

All Glory, Laud, and Honor

Theodulf of Orleans (c. 820)

Translated by John Mason Neale (1851)

All glory, laud and honor, To Thee, Redeemer, King, To Whom the lips of children Made sweet hosannas ring. Thou art the King of Israel, Thou David's royal Son, Who in the Lord's Name comest, The King and Blessed One.

All glory, laud and honor, To Thee, Redeemer, King, To Whom the lips of children Made sweet hosannas ring. The company of angels Are praising Thee on High, And mortal men and all things Created make reply.

All glory, laud and honor, To Thee, Redeemer, King, To Whom the lips of children Made sweet hosannas ring. The people of the Hebrews With palms before Thee went; Our prayer and praise and anthems Before Thee we present.

All glory, laud and honor, To Thee, Redeemer, King, To Whom the lips of children Made sweet hosannas ring. To Thee, before Thy passion, They sang their hymns of praise; To Thee, now high exalted, Our melody we raise.

All glory, laud and honor, To Thee, Redeemer, King, To Whom the lips of children Made sweet hosannas ring. Thou didst accept their praises; Accept the prayers we bring, Who in all good delightest, Thou good and gracious King.